Connect *with* **English**

VIDEO COMPREHENSION BOOK 3

Pamela McPartland-Fairman • Michael Berman • Linda Butler • Maggie Sokolik

McGraw Hill

Boston, Massachusetts   Burr Ridge, Illinois   Dubuque, Iowa   Madison, Wisconsin
New York, New York   San Francisco, California   St. Louis, Missouri

McGraw-Hill

A Division of The McGraw·Hill Companies

CONNECT WITH ENGLISH: VIDEO COMPREHENSION BOOK 3

This book is printed on acid-free paper.

domestic 1 2 3 4 5 6 7 8 9 0 QPD QPD 9 0 0 9 8 7
international 1 2 3 4 5 6 7 8 9 0 QPD QPD 9 0 0 9 8 7

ISBN 0-07-292760-7

Editorial director: Thalia Dorwick
Publisher: Tim Stookesberry
Development editor: Pam Tiberia
Production supervisor: Michelle Lyon
Print materials consultant: Marilyn Rosenthal
Project manager: Kate Gartner, Function Thru Form, Inc.
Design and Electronic Production: Function Thru Form, Inc.
Typeface: Frutiger
Printer and Binder: Quebecor Press Dubuque

Grateful acknowledgment is made for use of the following:

Still photography: Jeffrey Dunn, Ron Gordon, Judy Mason, Margaret Storm

Additional photographs: Episode 26 — Page 7 © Bill Horsman / Stock Boston; *Episode 30* — Page 2 © Dion Ogust / The Image Works; 7 © Myrleen Ferguson / Photo Edit; *Episode 31* — Page 2 © Uniphoto; 7 left © Bill Bachmann / Stock Boston; 7 right © James Blank / Stock Boston; *Episode 32* — Page 7 left © Joseph Sohm / Stock Boston; 7 right © Michael Newman / Photo Edit; *Episode 33* — Page 7 © Bob Daemmrich / Stock Boston; *Episode 35* — Page 2 © Michael Newman / Photo Edit; 7 © Mary Kate Denny / Photo Edit; *Episode 36* — Page 2 © David Ulmer / Stock Boston; 7 © Jim Pickerell / The Image Works

Illustrations: Episode 25 — p. 3, Meryl Treatner; *Episode 26* — p. 7, Bill Colrus; *Episode 27* — p. 7, Janice Fried; *Episode 29* — p. 3, Dave Sullivan; *Episode 32* — p. 7, Lisa Goldrick; *Episode 34* — p. 7, Janice Fried

Library of Congress Catalog Card Number: 97-74213

http://www.mhhe.com

TABLE OF CONTENTS

TO THE TEACHER

The primary goal of each *Video Comprehension Book* is to help students build listening comprehension skills and gain a clear understanding of the characters and story line in the *Connect with English* video series.

This Introduction and the following Visual Tour provide important information on how each *Video Comprehension Book* and the corresponding video episodes can be successfully combined to teach English as a second or foreign language.

PROFICIENCY LEVEL:

The comprehension exercises found in each *Video Comprehension Book* are accessible to high-beginning through intermediate students. While the majority of the activities are written at the high-beginning level, special *What About You?* features found throughout the books allow teachers to raise or lower the level of difficulty of the materials according to their students' abilities. These *What About You?* activities encourage students to share their personal opinions and ideas related to the characters and the story. Many times, students are asked to predict what they think will happen next. Because of the open-ended nature of these activities, there are numerous opportunities for classroom discussion and debates. The *What About You?* feature can also be used as the basis for writing and journal activities, creating further possibilities for exploration of themes related to the *Connect with English* story.

LANGUAGE SKILLS:

The primary skill emphasized in each *Video Comprehension Book* is listening, along with recognition skills related to facial expressions, body language, and cultural nuances. Additional language skills/topics covered in each book include reading, oral communication, and vocabulary development.

OPTIONS FOR USE:

Each *Video Comprehension Book* can be used in a variety of different learning environments, including classroom, distance learning, tutorial, and/or independent study situations. Instructors may choose to show the video during class time, while simultaneously using the *Video Comprehension Book*. If access to televisions or VCRs is not possible, teachers can assign students to watch the video episodes in a library, language lab, or at home. Class time can then be used for review of the activities found in the *Video Comprehension Book*.

The *Video Comprehension Books* can easily be combined with other corresponding texts in the *Connect with English* print program. For classes with an emphasis on oral communication skills, *Conversation Books 1-4* contain a variety of multi-level pair, group, team, and whole-class activities based on important themes and events from each episode. For classes with a focus on grammatical structures, *Grammar Guides 1-4* provide multi-level practice in grammar and vocabulary and also include various options for reading and writing activities. Finally, there are 16 *Connections Readers* which offer students graded reading practice based on the *Connect with English* story. For additional information about the *Connect with English* print program, please refer to the inside back cover of this book.

A VISUAL TOUR

The Opening Page

The first page of each chapter introduces key characters and themes from the corresponding video episode and builds on students' prior knowledge to help them predict upcoming events.

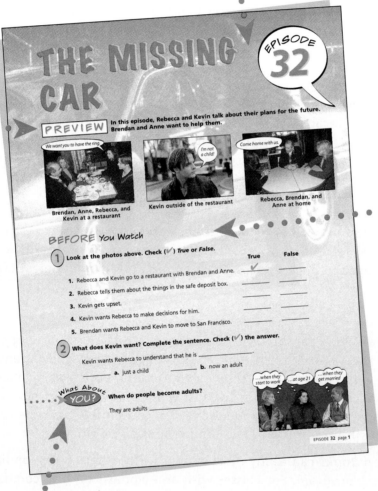

PREVIEW

This section presents a brief summary of the video episode. The three photos highlight key events from each of the three parts of the episode. The **Preview** section builds students' confidence as it gives them a base of contextualized clues about the characters and story line before they watch the video.

BEFORE You Watch

Activities in this section help students further identify the characters and story line. This particular example is a true / false activity which utilizes students' prior knowledge and calls upon their ability to make inferences about the information presented in the photos, captions, and speech bubbles on this page.

What About You? activities provide open-ended questions that encourage students to express their personal feelings, opinions, and reactions to the events and characters in the story. Whenever possible, language prompts or cues are used to provide linguistic support for lower-level students. At the same time, these activities create a springboard for more sophisticated discussions among students who are at higher levels of oral proficiency. The **What About You?** activities can also be used as optional writing assignments.

WATCH FOR MAIN IDEAS

This first viewing activity asks students to watch the entire episode with the purpose of focusing on major story highlights.

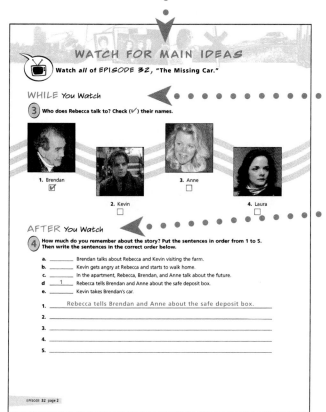

WHILE You Watch

The **While You Watch** section provides a focused viewing activity dealing with specific people, places, things, and/or events central to the development of the story.

AFTER You Watch

Activities in the **After You Watch** section ask students to recall specific information about the story. The first activity is usually a sequencing exercise dealing with the order of the major events in the episode. Many of the activities in this section also include an emphasis on recognition skills for facial expressions, body language, and cultural nuances.

Variety of Activity Types

A variety of different types of activities are included in each chapter, including multiple-choice, sentence completion, true/false, circling, and checking activities. The numbered activities are designed to be accessible to students engaged in independent study — at home, in a language lab, or any place where they have access to a TV and VCR. However, instructors can modify most of these activities into much more elaborate conversation and/or writing topics. For example, in the first sentence in Activity 5, we learn that Rebecca does not want Kevin to live with his friends. In a classroom setting, instructors can start a discussion by simply asking the question, *"Why?"*

---

5 **What do these people want? Check (✔) Yes or No.**

	Yes	No
1. Does Rebecca want Kevin to live with his friends?	_____	✔
2. Does Kevin want Rebecca to decide what he should do?	_____	_____
3. Does Brendan want Kevin to take the car?	_____	_____
4. Do Brendan and Anne want to help Rebecca and Kevin?	_____	_____
5. Do they want to give money to Rebecca and Kevin?	_____	_____

6 **Who is Laura? Complete the sentence. Check (✔) the answer.**

Laura is _____ .

_____ **a.** the Caseys' neighbor   _____ **b.** Kevin's girlfriend   _____ **c.** Rebecca's friend

What About YOU? **What do you think will happen? Check (✔) Yes or No.**

	Yes	No
1. Will Brendan find out the car is gone?	_____	_____
2. Will Kevin come home safe?	_____	_____
3. Will Rebecca and Kevin go to the farm?	_____	_____

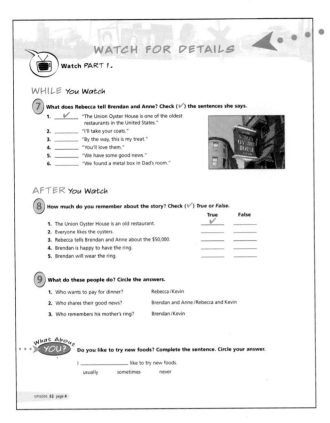

WATCH FOR DETAILS

Watch PART 1.

WHILE You Watch

7 What does Rebecca tell Brendan and Anne? Check (✔) the sentences she says.

1. ✔ "The Union Oyster House is one of the oldest restaurants in the United States."
2. _____ "I'll take your coats."
3. _____ "By the way, this is my treat."
4. _____ "You'll love them."
5. _____ "We have some good news."
6. _____ "We found a metal box in Dad's room."

AFTER You Watch

8 How much do you remember about the story? Check (✔) True or False.

	True	False
1. The Union Oyster House is an old restaurant.	✔	
2. Everyone likes the oysters.		
3. Rebecca tells Brendan and Anne about the $50,000.		
4. Brendan is happy to have the ring.		
5. Brendan will wear the ring.		

9 What do these people do? Circle the answers.

1. Who wants to pay for dinner? Rebecca/Kevin
2. Who shares their good news? Brendan and Anne/Rebecca and Kevin
3. Who remembers his mother's ring? Brendan/Kevin

What About YOU? Do you like to try new foods? Complete the sentence. Circle your answer.

I _____ like to try new foods.
usually   sometimes   never

EPISODE 32 page 4

WATCH FOR DETAILS

The **Watch for Details** section helps students develop a more specific understanding of the video story. Each video episode is divided into three viewing sections, labeled on-screen as Part 1, Part 2, and Part 3. In this section of the book, students are asked to view one part at a time, and comprehension is checked with more detailed activities regarding the characters and their experiences.

WHILE You Watch

Many of the **While You Watch** activities in *Video Comprehension Book 3* require students to listen and watch carefully in order to identify speakers, key vocabulary, or completed actions or events. In this example, students listen for specific lines spoken by each character, giving them practice in listening for details.

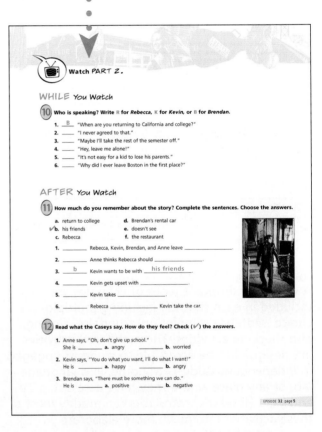

Watch PART 2.

WHILE You Watch

10 Who is speaking? Write **R** for Rebecca, **K** for Kevin, or **B** for Brendan.

1. __B__ "When are you returning to California and college?"
2. _____ "I never agreed to that."
3. _____ "Maybe I'll take the rest of the semester off."
4. _____ "Hey, leave me alone!"
5. _____ "It's not easy for a kid to lose his parents."
6. _____ "Why did I ever leave Boston in the first place?"

AFTER You Watch

11 How much do you remember about the story? Complete the sentences. Choose the answers.

a. return to college   d. Brendan's rental car
✔b. his friends   e. doesn't see
c. Rebecca   f. the restaurant

1. _____ Rebecca, Kevin, Brendan, and Anne leave _____
2. _____ Anne thinks Rebecca should _____
3. __b__ Kevin wants to be with _his friends_
4. _____ Kevin gets upset with _____
5. _____ Kevin takes _____
6. _____ Rebecca _____ Kevin take the car.

12 Read what the Caseys say. How do they feel? Check (✔) the answers.

1. Anne says, "Oh, don't give up school."
   She is _____ **a.** angry   _____ **b.** worried
2. Kevin says, "You do what you want, I'll do what I want!"
   He is _____ **a.** happy   _____ **b.** angry
3. Brendan says, "There must be something we can do."
   He is _____ **a.** positive   _____ **b.** negative

EPISODE 32 page 5

AFTER You Watch

The **After You Watch** activities continue to check students' comprehension of the story and help to solidify their understanding of the subtle nuances related to the characters' feelings and emotions.

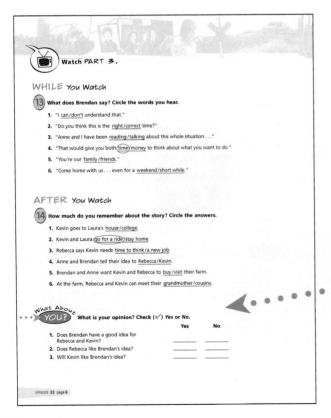

Watch PART 3.

WHILE You Watch

13 What does Brendan say? Circle the words you hear.

1. "I can/don't understand that."
2. "Do you think this is the right/correct time?"
3. "Anne and I have been reading/talking about this whole situation . . ."
4. "That would give you both time/money to think about what you want to do."
5. "You're our family/friends."
6. "Come home with us . . . even for a weekend/short while."

AFTER You Watch

14 How much do you remember about the story? Circle the answers.

1. Kevin goes to Laura's house/college.
2. Kevin and Laura go for a ride/stay home.
3. Rebecca says Kevin needs time to think/a new job.
4. Anne and Brendan tell their idea to Rebecca/Kevin.
5. Brendan and Anne want Kevin and Rebecca to buy/visit their farm.
6. At the farm, Rebecca and Kevin can meet their grandmother/cousins.

What About YOU? What is your opinion? Check (✔) Yes or No.

	Yes	No
1. Does Brendan have a good idea for Rebecca and Kevin?		
2. Does Rebecca like Brendan's idea?		
3. Will Kevin like Brendan's idea?		

EPISODE 32 page 6

Discussion Topics Encourage Conversation

The **What About You?** activity shown here asks students to share their opinions on certain issues occurring in this episode. These questions can be used as a basis for in-class discussions in which students discuss and compare their impressions of the events in the story.

HIGHLIGHTS

The **Highlights** page offers students an opportunity to explore various cultural and language points from the story.

CULTURE

These boxes expand on subject matter found in the video by providing cultural information about life in the United States and Canada. In this example, students learn about different ways that people choose to pay restaurant bills. An open-ended **What About You?** activity always follows the culture point and encourages students to compare and contrast their understanding of this new information with the corresponding cultural situation in their own countries.

EXPRESSIONS

In this section, students have an opportunity to work with some of the key idioms and expressions from the episode. Only those expressions which were presented in the context of the video story are included in this section. Care has been taken to ensure that the vocabulary features high-frequency items that students might encounter in conversational American English.

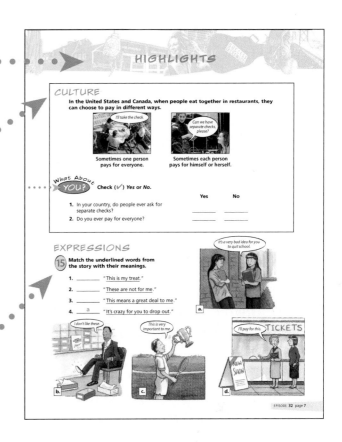

REVIEW AND DISCUSS

This final page of each chapter gives students the opportunity to review the entire episode and offers a chapter-culminating discussion topic.

STORY SUMMARY

In this section, students summarize the episode by selecting and inserting key vocabulary used in the video or earlier in the chapter. As in every exercise in the chapter, a sample answer is provided.

VIEWPOINTS

Activities found in the **Viewpoints** section are based on the final review portion of the video episode. In this part of the video, various non-native English speakers from around the world talk about the episode and share their personal feelings about things that happened. Students using *Video Comprehension Book 3* are asked to interpret and react to these comments and ideas in a final **What About You?** activity.

HOW TO USE THIS BOOK

CONNECT WITH ENGLISH is a story to help you learn English. Watch the program by yourself, in a classroom, or with family or friends. Record the program so you can watch it again. The episodes are closed-captioned. Turn on your caption system to see the words on the screen and get extra help in following the story.

This book will help you understand the story. Each episode has three parts. Before you watch the episode, look at the pictures in the *Preview* section. These pictures will show you some of the most important events from each part of the episode. The activities underneath the pictures will also help you get ready to watch.

Watch the episodes as many times as you need to. If you can, watch the whole episode one time through. Then you can go back and watch each part of the episode again. As you watch, you will see on-screen labels that say Part 1, Part 2, and Part 3. At the end of each episode, you will also see a group of students talk about the story.

The activities in the *Watch for the Main Ideas* and the *Watch for the Details* sections will help you learn the most important things that happen in each episode.

When you see a *What About You?* activity, you have a chance to talk about your own ideas and opinions about the **Connect with English** story. Discuss the questions and answers with your friends, family, or classmates. Your teacher might even ask you to write about your ideas.

In the *Highlights* section, a *Culture* box will tell you about life in the United States and Canada. In this section, you will also have a chance to talk about your country and how it is similar to or different from what you have learned about the United States and Canada. The *Expressions* section will help you understand some common American English phrases and expressions that the characters say in the episode.

On the last page of every chapter, a *Story Summary* reviews everything that happened in the episode. Look back through the activities you have already completed for help in doing the summary. The *Viewpoints* section gives you a chance to hear what some other English students think about **Connect with English**.

Remember, as you use this book, here's how you can *connect* with English: watch and record the episodes, read the book, and talk about the program with your family, friends, or classmates. Most of all, have fun and enjoy the story!

THE STORY SO FAR

1. Rebecca Casey is a singer. She lives in Boston with her brother, Kevin, and her father, Patrick.

2. Rebecca is very happy when she is accepted to the San Francisco College of Music.

3. Rebecca has car trouble on the way to San Francisco. She gets help from a man named Alberto. He is from San Francisco.

4. In San Francisco, Rebecca stays with her godmother, Nancy Shaw. Nancy rents rooms to other students.

5. Rebecca needs a job to pay for rent and school. She doesn't have any luck at her interviews.

6. Alberto and Rebecca go on a date. Rebecca meets Alberto's parents and his brother, Ramón.

7. Rebecca gets a job at an after-school program. She meets Ramón's son, Alex, and Alex's best friend, Vincent.

8. Rebecca talks to her father on the phone. She worries about his health.

9. Rebecca and Ramón become very good friends. Ramón tells Rebecca that his ex-wife Christine is moving to Los Angeles. Christine wants to take Alex with her.

10. The after-school program has a picnic. Some boys call Vincent names because he is Asian-American.

11. Rebecca and Emma teach the children about prejudice. Vincent's parents won't let Vincent come back to the program.

12. Rebecca wants to give Alex and Vincent free guitar lessons. She goes to Mrs. Wang's house to talk to her about it.

13. Ramón tells Alex that his mother wants to take him to Los Angeles. Alex gets angry at his father.

14. At Mr. and Mrs. Mendoza's retirement party, Alex tells Rebecca that he doesn't want to move to Los Angeles.

15. Nancy and Angela come to the party with some bad news about Rebecca's father. He is in the hospital.

LOOKING AHEAD

In this part of the story, Rebecca goes home to Boston. She meets her uncle Brendan for the first time. Rebecca and Kevin have to make some important decisions about their future. Rebecca's friend Sandy needs their help.

What About YOU? **What is your opinion? Check (✔) *Yes* or *No*.**

	Yes	No
1. Is Rebecca's father going to be OK?	_____	_____
2. Should Ramón let Alex move to Los Angeles?	_____	_____
3. Will Rebecca ever go back to San Francisco?	_____	_____

REBECCA REMEMBERS

| PREVIEW | In this episode, Rebecca is flying to Boston. She is very worried about her father. She thinks about her family and friends. |

Rebecca on the plane

Here's to the beginning of a new life!

Rebecca remembers Nancy's house

I love you, Dad.

Rebecca remembers her father at home

BEFORE You Watch

1 Look at the photos above. Complete the sentences. Choose the answers.

1. ____a____ Rebecca is _on the plane_____.

   a. on the plane   **b.** at school   **c.** at the hospital

2. ____b____ She is _thinking_____.

   a. watching a movie   **b.** thinking   **c.** reading a book

3. ____a____ Rebecca remembers meeting _the people at Nancy's house_.

   a. the people at Nancy's house   **b.** Bill   **c.** Alberto

4. ____c____ Rebecca thinks about _her father_____.

   a. Sandy   **b.** Kevin   **c.** her father

What About YOU?

What do you usually do when you travel?

I usually _____.

...read   *...sleep*   *...talk to people*

WATCH FOR MAIN IDEAS

Watch *all* of EPISODE 25, "Rebecca Remembers."

WHILE You Watch

2 **What does Rebecca remember? Circle the answers.**

1.

a. the Mendozas' party
b. meeting Alberto in the desert

2.

a. going to music school
b. giving guitar lessons

3.

a. playing softball with Alex
b. helping Alex study for a test

4.

a. talking to Ramón
b. dancing with Ramón

5.

a. Kevin telling her to stay in Boston
b. Kevin telling her to go to San Francisco

AFTER You Watch

3 **How much do you remember about the story? Check (✔) *True* or *False*.**

	True	False
1. Rebecca is on the plane to Chicago.		✓
2. She remembers getting bad news about her father.	✓	
3. Rebecca thinks about driving from Boston to San Francisco.		✔
4. Rebecca remembers her first dinner at Nancy's house.	✓	
5. She thinks about music school, and about her job.	✓	
6. Rebecca remembers talking with her Dad on the phone.	✓	
7. She knows she was right to leave Boston.	✓	
8. She knows that her family didn't want her to go to school.	✓	

4 How does Rebecca feel? Check (✔) the sentences that are true.

1. _____ She is happy and relaxed.

2. __✔__ She is worried about her father.

3. _____ She doesn't want to go back to Boston.

4. __✔__ She is frightened about the future.

5 What does Rebecca want? Circle the answer.

 **What do you think will happen? Check (✔) Yes or No.**

	Yes	No
1. Will Rebecca's father get better?		✔
2. Will Rebecca go back to San Francisco?	✔	

Watch PART 1.

WHILE You Watch

6 Listen to Rebecca's conversations with Nancy, Ramón, and Kevin. Circle the words you hear.

1. Rebecca: "What is it / wrong?"

2. Nancy: "It's your father. He's very sick / in the hospital."

3. Rebecca: "I have to call / go home. May I use your phone?"

4. Ramón: "Of course. There's a phone in the restaurant / kitchen."

5. Rebecca: "Is he OK? What did the nurse / doctor say?"

AFTER You Watch

7 How much do you remember about the story? Put the sentences in order from 1 to 5. Then write the sentences in the correct order below.

a. ___2___ Rebecca remembers Nancy coming to find her at the party.

b. ___1___ Rebecca is flying home to Boston.

c. ___3___ Rebecca remembers asking Ramón to use the phone.

d. ___5___ Rebecca is sorry she had to leave the Mendozas' party.

e. ___4___ Rebecca remembers calling Kevin about their father.

1. _____Rebecca is flying home to Boston._____

2. _Rebecca remembers Nancy coming to find her at the party._

3. _Rebecca remembers asking Ramón to use the phone._

4. _Rebecca remembers calling Kevin about their father._

5. _Rebecca is sorry she had to leave the Mendozas party._

6. _____

What is your opinion? Check (✔) I agree or I disagree.

	I agree	I disagree
1. Nancy should go to Boston with Rebecca.		✔
2. The Mendoza family is worried about Rebecca.	✔	

Watch PART **2.**

WHILE *You Watch*

8 **What places do you see? Check (✔) all the answers.**

1. the music school

✔

2. the Casa Mendoza restaurant

✔

3. the after-school program

✔

4. the art gallery

✔

5. the Caseys' apartment

✔

AFTER *You Watch*

9 **How much do you remember about the story?**
Use the words in the box to complete the sentences.

dinner✓   job✓   music✓   photographs   present ✔study

1. Rebecca remembers her first ___dinner___ at Nancy Shaw's house.

2. She thinks about meeting Bill at ___music___ school.

3. Rebecca remembers getting her ___job___ at the after-school program.

4. She remembers seeing Alberto's ___photographs___ at the art gallery.

5. She remembers getting a ___present___ from Mrs. Wang.

6. She thinks about helping Alex ___study___ for a test.

10 **What do you know about Rebecca? Check (✔) the sentences that *are not* true.**

1. ___✓___ Rebecca likes Alberto's photographs.

2. ___✔___ She doesn't like Mrs. Wang's present.

3. ___✓___ She wants to help Alex study.

4. _____ She says she is a great dancer.

 Watch PART 3.

WHILE You Watch

11 **Who is speaking? Write R for *Rebecca*, or P for *Patrick Casey*.**

1. __R__ "Are you all right?"
2. __P__ "Just a frog in my throat."
3. __P__ "So, how's school?"
4. __R__ "It's a lot of work."
5. __P__ "What do you want from me?"
6. __R__ "Just your approval."
7. __R__ "Thanks for everything."
8. __R__ "I love you."

AFTER You Watch

12 **How much do you remember about the story? Circle the answers.**

1. Rebecca remembers her father (coughing)/yelling on the phone.

2. She remembers her father saying that he's (OK)/very sick .

3. Rebecca remembers that Sandy thought music school was a (good)/bad idea.

4. Rebecca remembers that Kevin wanted her to (go to school)/stay in Boston .

5. Rebecca (is)/isn't worried about Kevin and her father.

6. She wonders why she left Boston/San Francisco .

7. She wonders what she will find when she gets (home)/to work .

What About YOU? **What do you think will happen? Circle your answers.**

1. Kevin will/won't be happy to see Rebecca.

2. Rebecca's father will be feeling better/worse when she gets home.

CULTURE

In the United States and Canada, the telephone is a popular way to communicate. Family and friends call each other often to talk, even if there is no emergency or important information to share. Writing letters is less common than using the telephone, but many people now use computers to send electronic letters via e-mail.

School? It's pretty tough, Dad. It's a lot of work.

What About YOU?

1. In your country, what do people do more often—write letters or talk on the phone?

_____

2. Do many people use e-mail to send letters?

_____

3. Which do you prefer—using the phone, writing letters, or sending e-mail?

_____

EXPRESSIONS

13 **Match the underlined words from the story with their meanings. Choose the answers.**

1. ____a____ The Narrator: "Mr. and Mrs. Mendoza are the <u>guests of honor</u> at the party."

    a. most important people   **b.** oldest people   **c.** richest people

2. _____ Alex: "<u>How come</u> you have books?"

    a. Why do   **b.** Where do   **c.** When do

3. ____c____ Rebecca: "School? It's pretty <u>tough</u>, Dad."

    a. ugly   **b.** easy   **c.** hard

4. ____a____ Rebecca: "<u>Oh my gosh</u>! It's me!"

    a. What a surprise!   **b.** It's ugly!   **c.** Hello!

REVIEW AND DISCUSS

STORY SUMMARY

14 Use the words in the box to complete the story summary for Episode 25.

✔back	children ✔	family ✔	father ✔	find ✔	friends ✔
✔hospital	house ✔	job ✔	party ✔	school ✔	thinks ✔	worried ✔

Rebecca is flying ___**back**___ (1) to Boston. She is very ___worried___ (2) about her father.

He is in the ___hospital___ (3). As she travels, she ___thinks___ (4) about her life in San Francisco.

She thinks about the Mendozas' retirement ___party___ (5), and about Alberto, Ramón, and

Alex. Rebecca remembers Nancy Shaw's ___house___ (6) and her ___friend___ (7) there. She

thinks about Bill and her friends at music ___school___ (8). Rebecca remembers getting her

___job___ (9) at the after-school program. She thinks about Emma Washington, and about the

___Children___ (10) at the program. Then Rebecca thinks about her ___father___ (11) again. She

remembers her ___family___ (12) and friends in Boston. She wonders why she left Boston. She

wonders what she will ___find___ (13) when she gets there.

VIEWPOINTS

15 Read what the narrator says about Rebecca. Check (✔) *True* or *False*.

	True	False
1. Rebecca thinks that she should have paid more attention to her father's health.	✔	
2. Rebecca always knew that her father was very sick.		✔

"*All of it was overwhelming. Did she neglect her family in Boston? Did she miss signs that something was wrong?*"

What About YOU? What is your opinion? Check (✔) *Yes* or *No*.

	Yes	No
1. Should Rebecca feel guilty about what happened to her father?		
2. Should Rebecca be angry at her father for not telling her that he was sick ?		

THE EMERGENCY

PREVIEW   In this episode, Rebecca returns to Boston. She goes to the hospital to see her father.

Hold on, Dad.

Mr. Casey and Kevin at home

You're going to be all right, you hear me?

Rebecca and her father at the hospital

I can't believe this!

Kevin and Rebecca at home

BEFORE You Watch

1   **Look at the photos above. Circle the answers.**

1. Mr. Casey has a ~~heart attack~~ / car accident .

2. Kevin / <u>Rebecca</u> is at home to help Mr. Casey.

3. Mr. Casey goes to the <u>hospital</u> / doctor's office .

4. Rebecca <u>is</u> / isn't worried about her father.

5. Rebecca and <u>her father</u> / Kevin go back to the apartment.

6. The apartment is clean / <u>messy</u> .

What About YOU?

Who would you call in an emergency?

I would call _____ .

Have you ever had an emergency?

...the police   *...911*   *...my brother*

WATCH FOR MAIN IDEAS

 Watch *all* of EPISODE 26, "The Emergency."

WHILE You Watch

2 **Who does Rebecca talk to? Check (✔) all the answers.**

1. Kevin
✔

2. an EMT*

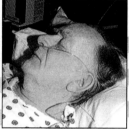

3. her father
☐

4. a doctor
☐

5. Mrs. Smith
☐

*EMT = emergency medical technician

AFTER You Watch

3 **How much do you remember about the story? Put the sentences in order from 1 to 5. Then write the sentences in the correct order below.**

a. _____ Rebecca and Kevin go home to rest.

b. _____ Rebecca and Kevin get a telephone call at home.

c. _____ Rebecca goes to see her father.

d. ___1___ Mr. Casey has a serious heart attack.

e. _____ Kevin calls 911 for help.

1. 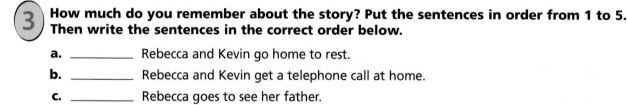 Mr. Casey has a serious heart attack.

2. _____

3. _____

4. _____

5. _____

4 What do you know about Kevin? Check (✔) *Yes* or *No*.

		Yes	No
1.	Is Kevin scared about his father's heart attack?	✔	
2.	Does Kevin call for help quickly?		
3.	Does Kevin know a lot about his father's medicine?		
4.	Is he happy to see Rebecca at the airport?		
5.	Does Kevin ask the doctor questions?		
6.	Is Kevin worried about his father?		

5 What does Rebecca do? Check (✔) the sentences that *are not* true.

1. _____✔_____ Rebecca takes a bus to the hospital.

2. _____ In the hospital, Rebecca talks to her father.

3. _____ Rebecca calls Aunt Molly.

4. _____ Rebecca goes home with Kevin.

5. _____ Rebecca gets angry about the messy apartment.

6. _____ Rebecca and Kevin go out to eat.

 **What do you think will happen? Check (✔) *Yes* or *No*.**

		Yes	No
1.	Will Mr. Casey get well?		
2.	Will Rebecca decide to stay in Boston?		

WATCH FOR DETAILS

 Watch PART 1.

WHILE You Watch

6 What information does Kevin give on the phone? Check (✔) the sentences he says.

1. _____ "This is Kevin Casey. . . I need an ambulance."

2. ___✔___ "I'm at 1097 E Street, apartment 3."

3. _____ "What part of the city is that?"

4. _____ "He's breathing, but barely."

5. _____ "OK, does he have any medical problems?"

6. _____ "He has a bad heart, and he has high blood pressure."

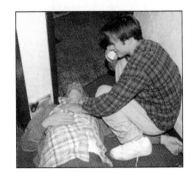

AFTER You Watch

7 How much do you remember about the story?
Use the words in the box to complete the sentences.

airport ✔chest floor heart attack help hospital

1. Mr. Casey feels a pain in his _____chest_____.

2. He falls on the _____.

3. Kevin calls 911 for _____.

4. At the _____, Kevin calls Rebecca.

5. He meets Rebecca at the _____.

6. He tells her about their father's _____.

8 How does Kevin feel? Complete the sentences. Choose the answers.

1. _____ When Kevin calls 911, he is _____.
   a. sad   **b.** upset   **c.** happy

2. _____ He is _____ about his father.
   a. excited   **b.** angry   **c.** worried

3. _____ He is _____ to see Rebecca.
   a. glad   **b.** sorry   **c.** angry

 Watch PART 2.

WHILE You Watch

9 **What does Rebecca say? Circle the words you hear.**

1. "I'm his sister / (daughter)."

2. "I'm back / home."

3. "Mom's ring / necklace, remember?"

4. "What does that say / mean?"

5. "Is he going to make it / die?"

6. "I think that I'd like to get / have a second opinion."

AFTER You Watch

10 **How much do you remember about the story? Circle the answers.**

1. Who takes Rebecca to Patrick's room?   (Kevin) / a nurse

2. Who holds Patrick's hand?   Rebecca / Kevin

3. Who tells Rebecca about Mr. Casey's condition? Kevin / Dr. Lincoln

4. Who asks the doctor some questions?   Rebecca / Kevin

11 **What do you know about Rebecca? Check (✔) Yes or No.**

	Yes	No
1. Is Rebecca wearing her mother's necklace?	✔	
2. Does Rebecca tell her father that he will be OK?		
3. Is Rebecca happy about what Dr. Lincoln says?		
4. Does Rebecca want to talk to another doctor?		

 **What is your opinion? Check (✔) I agree or I disagree.**

	I agree	I disagree
1. Rebecca thinks her father will get better.		
2. Mr. Casey is in a good hospital.		

Watch PART 3.

WHILE You Watch

12 Who is speaking? Write **R** for *Rebecca,* **K** for *Kevin,* or **S** for *Mrs. Smith.*

1. __R__ "Do you think I should call a priest?"
2. _____ "I'd like you to fill out a couple of forms for me."
3. _____ "Why didn't you call me?"
4. _____ "Don't blame me!"
5. _____ "We'll be right there."

AFTER You Watch

13 How much do you remember about the story? Check (✔) *True* or *False.*

	True	False
1. Kevin wants to call a priest.	_____	✔
2. Mrs. Smith wants information about Mr. Casey's insurance.	_____	_____
3. Rebecca finds a lot of food in the refrigerator.	_____	_____
4. Rebecca and Kevin have a fight.	_____	_____
5. Rebecca and Kevin go back to the hospital.	_____	_____

14 What does Rebecca say? Complete the sentences with the phrases below.

✔ **a.** go   **c.** believe this   **e.** do this later
  b. leave him   **d.** get some sleep   **f.** in the refrigerator

1. _____ "I don't want to _____."
2. _____ "My brother and I are going home. We need to _____."
3. _____ "Can we _____?"
4. _____ "I can't _____!"
5. _____ "There's no food _____!"
6. __a__ "It's Dad. We have to _____ go _____."

What About YOU? What is your opinion? Check (✔) *Yes* or *No.*

	Yes	No
1. Is a clean home important to you?	_____	_____
2. Should Rebecca be angry about the messy apartment?	_____	_____

CULTURE

In the United States, health care is very good but very expensive. Many Americans buy private health insurance. Health insurance helps pay doctor or hospital bills.

In Canada, there is a government health insurance program. All Canadians have health insurance.

a doctor's waiting room

 **Check (✔) Yes or No.**

	Yes	No
1. Should the government pay for health insurance?	_____	_____
2. Should everyone have health insurance?	_____	_____

EXPRESSIONS

15 Match the underlined words from the story with their meanings.

1. _____ "Hold on."

2. ___a___ "He's on medication."

3. _____ "I can handle it!"

4. _____ "We'll be right there."

He is taking medicine that his doctor gave him.

a.

We'll be there soon.

d.

Wait just a little. Help is coming.

b.

I can do it.

c.

REVIEW AND DISCUSS

STORY SUMMARY

16 Use the words in the box to complete the story summary for Episode 26.

✔arrives	doctor	empty	fight	hospital	meets	mess
news	rest	sees	serious	tells	wants	

Rebecca _____arrives_____ at the Boston airport, and Kevin _____ her there. On
(1)   (2)

the way to the _____, he _____ her about their father's heart attack. At
(3)   (4)

the hospital, Rebecca _____ her father. Then she talks to a _____. Patrick
(5)   (6)

Casey's condition is _____. Rebecca _____ a second opinion. She takes
(7)   (8)

Kevin home to _____. The apartment is a _____, and the refrigerator
(9)   (10)

is _____. She and Kevin have a _____. Then they get a phone call with
(11)   (12)

bad _____.
(13)

VIEWPOINTS

17 Watch the video discussion group. What does Laura mean?
Check (✔) *True* or *False*.

> The touch of a woman is missing.

	True	False
1. Laura is talking about the messy apartment.	_____	_____
2. She thinks men are messy.	_____	_____

Laura Eastment, Argentina

What About YOU?

What is your opinion? Check (✔) *I agree* or *I disagree*.

	I agree	I disagree
Men need women to take care of them.	_____	_____

BAD NEWS

PREVIEW   In this episode, Rebecca and Kevin meet Father O'Connor and Brendan Casey. Sandy comes to the hospital to see Rebecca.

I will begin my prayers for your father.

Father O'Connor at the hospital

I'll take the next flight out.

Brendan Casey at home

How are you doing?

Rebecca and Sandy at the hospital

BEFORE You Watch

1 **Look at the photos above. Complete the sentences. Choose the answers.**

1. ____a____ Father O'Connor is a __Catholic priest__.
   a. Catholic priest   **b.** doctor

2. _____ Brendan Casey will _____.
   a. go to Boston   **b.** stay at home

3. _____ Brendan _____ to see Patrick.
   a. wants   **b.** doesn't want

4. _____ Brendan lives _____.
   a. in Boston   **b.** far from Boston

5. _____ Sandy is _____ Rebecca.
   a. worried about   **b.** happy for

...my sister

...my parents

Who are you close to in your family?

I'm close to _____.

WATCH FOR MAIN IDEAS

 Watch *all* of EPISODE 27, "Bad News."

WHILE You Watch

2 Who comes to the hospital? Check (✔) their names.

1. a priest
☑

2. Sandy
☐

3. Aunt Molly
☐

4. Brendan
☐

5. Brendan's wife
☐

AFTER You Watch

3 How much do you remember about the story? Put the photos in order from 1 to 5.

a. _____

b. _____

c. ___1___

d. _____

e. _____

Did Jack hit you?

a.

What do the doctors say?

b.

At this point it does not look good.

c.

Hello. I'm Father O'Connor.

d.

Call my brother.

e.

4 **What do you know about Brendan Casey? Check (✔) _True_ or _False._**

	True	False
1. Brendan Casey is Patrick's uncle.	_____	✔
2. He is a farmer.	_____	_____
3. He is married.	_____	_____
4. Brendan and Patrick are very close.	_____	_____
5. Brendan is upset that Patrick is sick.	_____	_____

5 **What do you know about these people? Circle the answers.**

1. Who is angry at Rebecca?   (Kevin)/Sandy

2. Who gives Rebecca and Kevin the bad news?   Dr. Lincoln / Father O'Connor

3. Who tells Rebecca to take care of Kevin?   her father / her uncle

4. Who is very quiet?   Rebecca / Kevin

5. Who has bad bruises on her face?   Rebecca / Sandy

6 **How is Patrick Casey's health now? Complete the sentence. Check (✔) the answer.**

Patrick's health is _____.

_____ **a.** the same

_____ **b.** better

_____ **c.** worse

What About YOU? **What do you think will happen? Check (✔) _Yes_ or _No_.**

	Yes	No
1. Will Patrick talk to his brother?	_____	_____
2. Will Sandy tell Rebecca the truth?	_____	_____

WATCH FOR DETAILS

 Watch PART 1.

WHILE You Watch

7 **Listen to Rebecca's conversations at the hospital. Circle the words you hear.**

1. Dr. Lincoln: "At this point, it does not look (good)/serious."
2. Rebecca: "Aren't there any new drugs/medicines you can give him?"
3. Father O'Connor: "Tell me about your father's life/condition."
4. Rebecca: "My father and uncle don't talk to/care about each other."
5. Father O'Connor: "I will begin my prayers for your family/father."

AFTER You Watch

8 **How much do you remember about the story? Check (✔) Yes or No.**

	Yes	No
1. Is Rebecca sorry about the fight with Kevin?	✔	
2. Did Mr. Casey have a second heart attack?		
3. Can new drugs help Mr. Casey's heart now?		
4. Does Rebecca tell the priest about other people in the family?		
5. Does Father O'Connor want Rebecca to call Brendan?		

9 **Look at the words in the box. Find and circle them in the puzzle.**

emergency	family	heart	priest	✔ sorry	unhappy

```
I F A M I L Y X V
H M U N H A P P Y
E J O R E R R X P
A E F R Q F I E S
R G N Y S N E L O
T C F E Y S S C R
Y U X R B O T J R
E M E R G E N C Y
```

 **What is your opinion? Check (✔) I agree or I disagree.**

	I agree	I disagree
1. Dr. Lincoln is a good doctor.		
2. Father O'Connor can help Rebecca and Kevin.		

EPISODE **27** page 4

WHILE You Watch

10 Who is speaking? Write **R** for *Rebecca,* **B** for *Brendan,* or **P** for *Patrick.*

1. _____ "I'm afraid I have some bad news."

2. _____ "I'll take the next flight out."

3. _____ "Thank you for calling."

4. _P_ "Kevin, Kevin. Take care of Kevin."

5. _____ "Call my brother. Call Brendan."

6. _____ "Can you do something about the pain?"

AFTER You Watch

11 How much do you remember about the story? Put the sentences in order from 1 to 5. Then write the sentecnces in the correct order below.

a. _____ The priest comes in to pray.

b. ___1___ Rebecca calls her uncle.

c. _____ Mr. Casey asks Rebecca to call his brother.

d. _____ Brendan decides to go to Boston.

e. _____ The nurse gives Mr. Casey more pain medication.

1. _____ Rebecca calls her uncle. _____

2. _____

3. _____

4. _____

5. _____

12 What is Brendan thinking? Check (✔) the sentence that *is not* true.

_____ **a.** He is worried about Patrick.

_____ **b.** He is glad that Rebecca called him.

_____ **c.** He doesn't want to see Patrick.

Watch PART 3.

WHILE You Watch

13 **What do Rebecca and Sandy talk about? Check (✔) all the answers.**

1. ___✔___ Mr. Casey
2. _____ Kevin
3. _____ San Francisco
4. _____ Alberto
5. _____ Father O'Connor
6. _____ Jack

AFTER You Watch

14 **How much do you remember about the story? Check (✔) True or False.**

	True	False
1. Rebecca and Sandy go to get some coffee.	_____	_____
2. Sandy and Jack aren't living together.	_____	_____
3. There are bruises on Sandy's face.	___✔___	_____
4. Sandy had an accident.	_____	_____
5. Uncle Brendan is at the hospital now.	_____	_____

15 **How does Rebecca feel? Complete the sentences. Choose the answers.**

1. ___a___ Rebecca is _____surprised_____ to see Sandy at the hospital.
   a. surprised   **b.** angry

2. _____ Rebecca is _____ Kevin.
   a. angry at   **b.** worried about

3. _____ She is _____ to talk to Sandy.
   a. sorry   **b.** happy

4. _____ She is _____ Sandy's life.
   a. interested in   **b.** happy about

5. _____ Rebecca is _____ Jack.
   a. angry at   **b.** sorry for

What About YOU? **What is your opinion? Check (✔) Yes or No.**

	Yes	No
1. Sandy should leave Jack.	_____	_____
2. Rebecca wants to help Sandy.	_____	_____
3. Rebecca should talk to Jack.	_____	_____

CULTURE

In the United States and Canada, family members often live far apart. Sometimes they live hundreds or thousands of miles away from their relatives.

Parents and their young children usually live together. Sometimes a grandparent lives with them, too. Young adults often live with friends.

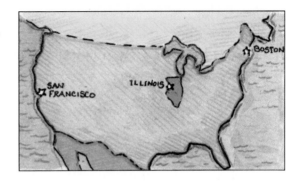

 **What About YOU?** Check (✔) *Yes* or *No*.

	Yes	No
1. Do you live with your parents?	_____	_____
2. Do you live with your grandparents?	_____	_____

EXPRESSIONS

16 **Match the underlined words from the story with their meanings.**

a. I will help you.

b. . . . immediately

c. . . . the most terrible thing I can think of

d. Something bad will probably happen.

e. That isn't going to happen now.

1. _____ Rebecca: ". . . <u>right away</u>."

2. _____ Dr. Lincoln: "<u>It does not look good</u>."

3. _____ Father O'Connor: "<u>I'm here for you</u>."

4. _____ Rebecca: ". . . <u>my worst nightmare</u>."

5. ___*e*___ Sandy: "<u>That's off</u>."

REVIEW AND DISCUSS

STORY SUMMARY

17 Use the words in the box to complete the story summary for Episode 27.

asks	brother	come	face	family	finds	heart
hit	✔hospital		see		tells	uncle

Rebecca and Kevin return to the ___hospital___ (1). Their father had a second

_____ (2) attack. A priest comes, and he _____ (3) about other

_____ (4) members. Patrick has a _____ (5), Brendan, but they stopped talking

many years ago. Rebecca calls her _____ (6). Brendan promises to _____ (7) right

away. Sandy comes to _____ (8) Rebecca. She has bruises on her _____ (9). She

_____ (10) Rebecca she had an accident, but Rebecca thinks Jack _____ (11) her.

Kevin _____ (12) Rebecca in the cafeteria. He tells her Uncle Brendan is there.

VIEWPOINTS

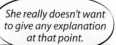

She really doesn't want to give any explanation at that point.

18 Watch the video discussion group. What does Abdul mean? Circle the answers.

1. Abdul is talking about Rebecca /Sandy.

2. He thinks Sandy tells /doesn't tell Rebecca the truth.

Abdul Khushafah, Yemen

What About YOU? What is your opinion? Check (✔) *I agree* or *I disagree*.

	I agree	I disagree
1. Sandy is embarrassed.	_____	_____
2. Sandy should tell Rebecca about her problems.	_____	_____

BROTHERS

PREVIEW In this episode, there is another emergency. Rebecca and Kevin meet Anne Casey, Brendan's wife.

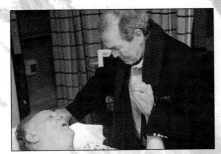

Patrick and Brendan
in Patrick's room

Nurse! Hurry! Help!

Brendan
at the hospital

Thank you for making the trip.

Anne, Brendan, and Rebecca
at the funeral home

BEFORE You Watch

1 **Look at the photos above. Check (✔) Yes or No.**

	Yes	No
1. Does Brendan see his brother?	✔	
2. Is Patrick feeling better?		
3. Does Patrick ask for help?		
4. Does Brendan's wife, Anne, come to Boston?		

2 **What do you know about Patrick Casey? Circle the answers.**

1. Patrick is in bad/good condition.

2. He wants/doesn't want to see his brother.

3. He stopped talking to Brendan many years/a few days ago.

What About YOU? **What is your opinion? Check (✔) Yes or No.**

	Yes	No
1. Was it a good idea for Rebecca to call her uncle?		
2. Is Patrick going to get better?		

Watch *all* of EPISODE 28, "Brothers."

WHILE You Watch

3 **What places do you see in the episode? Check (✔) all the answers.**

1. Patrick's hospital room
✔

2. the hospital cafeteria
☐

3. the Caseys' kitchen
☐

4. a restaurant
☐

5. a funeral home
☐

AFTER You Watch

4 **How much do you remember about the story? Write the sentences under the photos.**

a. "Begin CPR."

b. "I'm sorry I yelled at you."

✔**c.** "It's so good to meet you."

d. "I'm glad you came."

e. "I'm very sorry to hear about your father."

1. ___c___

2. _____

3. _____

4. _____

5. _____

1. Rebecca: "It's so good to meet you."

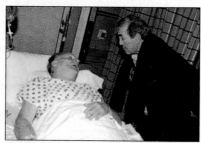

2. Patrick:_____

3. Rebecca:_____
_____

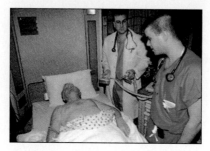

4. Doctor:_____
_____

5. Anne:_____
_____

5 **What do you know about these people? Use the words in the box to complete the sentences.**

brother	dies	happy	✔ meets	quiet	sorry

1. Rebecca _____meets_____ her uncle Brendan.

2. Brendan wants to see his _____ alone.

3. Rebecca is _____ about yelling at Kevin.

4. Patrick is _____ to see Brendan.

5. Rebecca is very sad when her father _____.

6. Kevin is _____. He doesn't talk much.

6 **Who does Rebecca call when her father dies? Check (✔) the answer.**

_____ **a.** Alberto

_____ **b.** Aunt Molly

_____ **c.** Anne Casey

What do you think will happen? Check (✔) Yes or No.

	Yes	No
1. Will Rebecca see Sandy?	_____	_____
2. Will Brendan tell Rebecca about the past?	_____	_____

Watch PART 1.

WHILE You Watch

7 **Who is speaking? Write K for Kevin, R for Rebecca, or B for Brendan.**

1. __B__ "Does he know you called me?"

2. _____ "Can I go in and see him?"

3. _____ "I hope we did the right thing."

4. _____ "I'll survive."

5. _____ "I'm going to go and say goodnight to Sandy."

AFTER You Watch

8 **How much do you remember about the story? Check (✔) *True* or *False*.**

	True	**False**
1. Rebecca and Kevin meet their uncle Brendan for the first time.	✔	
2. Brendan goes into Patrick's room with Rebecca.		
3. It is easy for Patrick to speak.		
4. Patrick and Brendan forgive each other.		
5. Sandy is waiting for Rebecca in the cafeteria.		

9 **What do you remember about Brendan and Patrick's conversation? Use the words in the box to complete the sentences.**

brother	✔ come	forget	glad	time

1. Brendan: "Patrick? Patrick . . . It's Brendan, your long lost _____."

2. Brendan: "Rebecca called me. She told me you asked for me to _____ come _____."

3. Patrick: "I'm _____ you came."

4. Brendan: "It's been a long _____ . . . too long, I guess."

5. Brendan: "I'm ready to forgive and _____. How about you?"

Watch PART 2.

WHILE You Watch

10 **What happens at the hospital? Circle the answers.**

1. Who gets angry about Jack?   Kevin / Brendan
2. Who cries?   Rebecca / Kevin
3. Who makes a phone call?   Rebecca / Brendan

AFTER You Watch

11 **How much do you remember about the story? Put the sentences in order from 1 to 5. Then write the sentences in the correct order below.**

a. _____ Brendan goes to get help.

b. _____ Patrick's heart stops.

c. ___1___ Rebecca tells Kevin about Sandy and Jack.

d. _____ The doctors try to help Patrick, but he dies.

e. _____ Brendan calls his wife with the bad news.

1. _____ Rebecca tells Kevin about Sandy and Jack. _____

2. _____

3. _____

4. _____

5. _____

12 **How does Kevin feel? Check (✔) Yes or No.**

	Yes	No
1. Is Kevin worried about Sandy?	_____	_____
2. Does he like Jack?	_____	_____
3. Is he upset about his father?	_____	_____

What About YOU? **What is your opinion? Check (✔) I agree or I disagree.**

	I agree	I disagree
1. Mr. Casey's doctors did a good job.	_____	_____
2. Kevin needs a friend.	_____	_____

 Watch PART 3.

WHILE You Watch

13 **What does Rebecca say? Circle the words you hear.**

1. "Dad passed away this (morning)/ afternoon."
2. "Dad's friend Frank Wells will call you / pick you up."
3. "It all happened so fast / soon."
4. "It's wrong for brothers / a family to be like that."
5. "Can I ask you something / a question?"

AFTER You Watch

14 **How much do you remember about the story? Complete the sentences with the words below.**

    a. to the funeral home   **d.** about her father
    b. Patrick and Brendan's fight   **e.** with Rebecca
✔ **c.** Aunt Molly

1. ____c____ Rebecca calls _____ Aunt Molly _____.
2. _____ Rebecca tells Molly _____.
3. _____ Alberto and Anne send flowers _____.
4. _____ Anne Casey sits and talks _____.
5. _____ Rebecca asks about _____.

15 **What do you know about Anne? Check (✔) the sentences that are true.**

1. ___✔___ She goes to the funeral home with Brendan.
2. _____ She says she is sorry about Rebecca's father.
3. _____ She cries because Patrick is dead.
4. _____ She says she is upset with Kevin.
5. _____ She doesn't tell Rebecca about Patrick and Brendan's fight.

 **What is your opinion? Check (✔) Yes or No.**

                                        Yes   **No**

1. Rebecca should ask Brendan about the fight. _____ _____
2. Brendan should tell Rebecca what happened. _____ _____

CULTURE

In the United States and Canada, when someone dies, it is the custom to send a card or write a letter to that person's family. People often send flowers, too.

Sometimes people want to remember the person in a different way. For example, if a person dies of cancer, a friend can give money to a group that helps people with cancer.

In your country, what do relatives and friends do when someone dies? Check (✔) your answers.

They _____ .

_____ visit the family   _____ write letters

_____ send flowers   _____ pray

_____ give food   _____ play music

_____ go to church   _____ wear different clothes

EXPRESSIONS

 Match the underlined words from the story with their meanings. Check (✔) the answers.

1. Brendan: "How are you holding up?"

   _____ **a.** What are you doing?
   ___✔___ **b.** How are you doing?

2. Rebecca: "She took off."

   _____ **a.** She left without waiting.
   _____ **b.** She got angry.

3. Kevin: "You have got to be kidding."

   _____ **a.** You have to be quiet.
   _____ **b.** I can't believe that is true.

4. Rebecca: "What's going on?"

   _____ **a.** What's happening?
   _____ **b.** What do you think?

5. Rebecca: "Dad passed away."

   _____ **a.** Dad died.
   _____ **b.** Dad went to sleep.

STORY SUMMARY

17 Use the words in the box to complete the story summary for Episode 28.

calls	come	dies	first	funeral
goes	✔meet	news	peace	see

Rebecca and Kevin ____meet____ their uncle for the _____ time. He asks to
(1)   (2)

_____ his brother alone, and he _____ into Patrick's room. The two
(3)   (4)

brothers make _____, and then Patrick _____. Brendan _____
(5)   (6)   (7)

his wife, Anne. He asks her to _____ to Boston for the funeral. Rebecca calls Aunt Molly
(8)

and other relatives with the sad_____. The next day they meet at a _____
(9)   (10)

home. There they hold a wake for Patrick.

VIEWPOINTS

18 Watch the video discussion group. What does Abdul mean?
Check (✔) *True* or *False*.

> *Disaster always brings the good out of human beings.*

	True	False
1. Abdul is talking about Patrick's heart attack.	_____	_____
2. He thinks it was good that the brothers talked.	_____	_____

**Abdul Khushafah,
Yemen**

What is your opinion? Check (✔) *I agree* or *I disagree*.

	I agree	I disagree
1. When bad things happen, people can learn good things.	_____	_____
2. Brothers and sisters often fight.	_____	_____
3. Fights between brothers and sisters usually are not serious.	_____	_____

GRIEF

PREVIEW In this episode, people speak about Patrick Casey at the wake and at the cemetery.

I'm presenting you with this helmet.

Kevin, Rebecca, and the
Boston fire chief at the wake

Where have you been? I've been worried about you!

Rebecca and Sandy
at the funeral home

May God bless and keep our brother Patrick Casey.

Brendan, Father O'Connor,
Rebecca, and Kevin
at the cemetery

BEFORE You Watch

1 Look at the photos above. Use the words in the box to complete the sentences.

father	✔ funeral home	gives	prayers	says	see

1. The fire chief _____ Rebecca a helmet.

2. The helmet is to honor and remember her _____.

3. Sandy comes to the ___funeral home___.

4. Rebecca is glad to _____ her there.

5. Father O'Connor _____ prayers at the cemetery.

6. Rebecca, Kevin, and Brendan listen to Father O'Connor's _____ for Patrick.

 **What is your opinion? Check (✔) *I agree* or *I disagree*.**

	I agree	I disagree
1. Patrick Casey had many friends.	_____	_____
2. He was an important person.	_____	_____

Watch *all* of EPISODE 29, "Grief."

WHILE You Watch

 2 Who makes a speech about Patrick Casey? Check (✔) their names.

1. the fire chief
☑

2. Frank Wells
☐

3. Kevin
☐

4. Rebecca
☐

5. Brendan
☐

AFTER You Watch

3 How much do you remember about the story? Put the photos in order from 1 to 6.

a. _____ b. _____ c. __1__ d. _____ e. _____ f. _____

My father had dreams.

a.

Are you going back?

b.

We'll have to be their family now.

c.

In recognition of your father's bravery ...

d.

Amen.

e.

He's promised never to do it again.

f.

4 **What do you know about Rebecca and Kevin? Check (✔) *True* or *False*.**

	True	False
1. Rebecca is surprised to see Matt.	✔	
2. Rebecca is happy to see Sandy.		
3. Rebecca is glad that Jack is with Sandy.		
4. It's hard for Kevin to talk about his father.		
5. Rebecca and Kevin think Patrick was a good father.		

5 **What did Patrick Casey always want? Circle the answer.**

a. ...*a big car*

b. ...*a small house with a garden*

c. ...*a fast boat*

 **What do you think will happen? Check (✔) *Yes* or *No*.**

	Yes	No
1. Will Sandy call Rebecca?		
2. Will Jack hit Sandy again?		

WATCH FOR DETAILS

 Watch PART 1.

WHILE You Watch

6 **Listen to Rebecca. Check (✔) the sentences she says.**

1. _____ "Matt! It's good to see you."
2. _____ "How's life in San Francisco?"
3. ___✔___ "School is tough, but I like it."
4. _____ "I've been worried about you."
5. _____ "I haven't been home."

AFTER You Watch

7 **How much do you remember about the story? Put the sentences in order from 1 to 5. Then write the sentences in the correct order below.**

a. _____ Matt comes to the wake to see Rebecca.
b. ___1___ Aunt Molly talks with Brendan and Anne.
c. _____ Frank Wells talks about his old friend.
d. _____ Sandy comes to the wake, but she can't stay.
e. _____ The fire chief gives Rebecca a helmet.

1. ___Aunt Molly talks with Brendan and Anne._____
2. _____
3. _____
4. _____
5. _____

8 **What do you know about these people? Complete the sentences. Choose the answers.**

1. ___b___ Aunt Molly is worried about ___Rebecca and Kevin___.
   a. Brendan and Anne   b. Rebecca and Kevin

2. _____ Frank Wells wants to _____.
   a. help Patrick's children   b. forget Patrick

3. _____ Matt is interested in Rebecca's _____.
   a. music   b. future plans

4. _____ Sandy still has a relationship with _____.
   a. Matt   b. Jack

Watch PART 2.

WHILE You Watch

 9 **What do Kevin and Rebecca say? Circle the words you hear.**

1. Kevin: "My father was a good man /(father)."

2. Kevin: "He had a big /good heart."

3. Kevin: "I'm /We're going to miss him."

4. Rebecca: "My father had problems /dreams."

5. Rebecca: "You always cared for /worried about us and loved us."

6. Rebecca: "I hope you find your dreams /happiness now."

AFTER You Watch

 10 **How much do you remember about the story? Check (✔) True or False.**

	True	False
1. Patrick's family and friends go to a park.	_____	✔
2. Father O'Connor says prayers for Patrick.	_____	_____
3. Kevin thinks that he made life hard for his father.	_____	_____
4. Rebecca talks about her father's problems.	_____	_____
5. She thinks that she disappointed her father.	_____	_____

11 **How do Rebecca and Kevin feel? Circle the answers.**

1. Kevin thinks his father had a (hard)/easy life.

2. Kevin is going to miss /forget his father.

3. Rebecca is sorry /worried that her father didn't find his dreams.

4. Rebecca and Kevin know /don't know that their father loved them.

Watch PART 3.

WHILE You Watch

12 Who talks about his or her family? Check (✔) their names.

1. Laura
✔

2. Lan
☐

3. Rosalba
☐

4. Olga
☐

5. Raúl
☐

AFTER You Watch

13 How much do you remember about the students? Check (✔) *Yes* or *No*.

	Yes	No
1. Did Laura's parents die?	✔	
2. Was Rosalba's father happy about her career in music?		
3. Did Olga's father die at home?		
4. Is Raúl's father living?		

14 What do the students say? Complete the sentences with the words below.

a. very guilty   **c.** passed away

✔**b.** my own experience   **d.** your family

1. ___b___ Laura: "This episode reminds me of _my own experience_."

2. _____ Rosalba: "I felt _____."

3. _____ Olga: "My father _____."

4. _____ Casilda: "It can't happen with _____."

 **In your country, what do people do when someone dies?**

In my country, when someone dies, people _____.

CULTURE

In the United States and Canada, when someone dies, the family and friends at the funeral often make speeches about the person's life. People talk about the good things that the person did and said.

 **What is your opinion?**
Check (✔) I agree or I disagree.

	I agree	I disagree
1. A funeral is a time to be sad and quiet.	_____	_____
2. A funeral is a time to talk about happy things.	_____	_____

EXPRESSIONS

 Match the underlined words from the story with their meanings. Check (✔) the answers.

1.

It's such a shame.

_____ **a.** It's too bad.

_____ **b.** It's a good thing.

2.

Call on me.

_____ **a.** Listen to me.

_____ **b.** Ask me for help.

3.

He had a big heart.

_____ **a.** He had heart problems.

_____ **b.** He was a good person.

REVIEW AND DISCUSS

STORY SUMMARY

 16 **Use the words in the box to complete the story summary for Episode 29.**

comes	dreams	father	friend	gives	✔Members
miss	plans	says	stay	talks	wake

_____Members_____ of the Boston Fire Department come to the _____. The fire chief
     (1)   (2)

_____ Rebecca a firefighter's helmet in honor of her _____. Frank Wells,
  (3)   (4)

Patrick's old _____, also speaks about him. Matt _____ to the wake,
             (5)   (6)

and he asks Rebecca about her _____. Sandy comes, too, but Jack doesn't let her
                               (7)

_____. At the cemetery, Father O'Connor _____ prayers for Patrick. Kevin
   (8)   (9)

_____ about his father. He will _____ him. Then Rebecca describes her
  (10)   (11)

father's _____. They never came true.
       (12)

VIEWPOINTS

I can't believe she is still with Jack.

17 **Watch the video discussion group. What does Casilda mean? Circle the answers.**

1. Casilda is talking about Rebecca / Sandy .

2. She is / isn't glad that Sandy is with Jack.

Casilda Nunes,
Brazil

What is your opinion? Check (✔) *I agree* or *I disagree.*

	I agree	I disagree
1. Sandy and Jack have a big problem.	_____	_____
2. There are many people like Sandy and Jack.	_____	_____

LIFE GOES ON

EPISODE **30**

PREVIEW **In this episode, Rebecca and Kevin talk about the future.**

① *You're going to go back to school, aren't you?*

② *I'd like that, but I feel responsible for Kevin.*

Anne, Brendan, and Rebecca in the kitchen

I'm not a baby.

Rebecca and Kevin in the neighborhood

How much do the bills add up to?

Rebecca and Kevin at home

BEFORE You Watch

① **Look at the photos above. Check (✔) Yes or No.**

	Yes	No
1. Is Anne interested in Rebecca's plans?	✔	
2. Does Rebecca want to go back to school?		
3. Does Rebecca worry about Kevin?		
4. Does Kevin think he needs Rebecca's help?		
5. Do Rebecca and Kevin have bills to pay?		

② **What kind of bills do you think Kevin and Rebecca have to pay? Check (✔) the answer that *is not* true.**

_____ **a.** some of their father's hospital bills

_____ **b.** their father's funeral expenses

_____ **c.** Uncle Brendan's plane ticket

What About YOU?

What do you do when you are unhappy?

When I am unhappy, I _____

_____

...talk about my feelings

...want to be alone

...go out and exercise

WATCH FOR MAIN IDEAS

 Watch *all* of **EPISODE 30**, "Life Goes On."

WHILE *You Watch*

3 What things do you see? Check (✔) all the answers.

1. a card
☑

2. food
☐

3. a mural
☐

4. a pizza
☐

5. a photo
☐

AFTER *You Watch*

4 How much do you remember about the story? Put the sentences in order from 1 to 5. Then write the sentences in the correct order below.

a. _____ Kevin and Rebecca look at the bills they have to pay.

b. _____ Frank Wells talks about Patrick and the funeral.

c. _____ Kevin tells Rebecca about the insurance policy.

d. ___1___ Anne and Brendan talk to Rebecca about Kevin.

e. _____ Rebecca asks Kevin about his plans.

1. _____Anne and Brendan talk to Rebecca about Kevin._____

2. _____

3. _____

4. _____

5. _____

5 **What do these people want? Check (✔) *True* or *False*.**

	True	False
1. Kevin wants to talk about his feelings.	_____	✔
2. Anne and Brendan want to help Kevin and Rebecca.	_____	_____
3. Anne and Brendan want to move to Boston.	_____	_____
4. Rebecca wants Kevin to go to college.	_____	_____
5. Kevin wants to go to San Francisco.	_____	_____
6. Kevin wants Rebecca to take care of him.	_____	_____

6 **What do you know about Rebecca and Kevin? Complete the sentences with *Rebecca, Kevin,* or *Rebecca and Kevin*.**

1. _____ reads cards from family and friends.

2. _____ talks with Brendan and Anne.

3. _____ adds up the bills.

4. _Rebecca and Kevin_ need money.

5. _____ remembers the insurance policy.

6. _____ go into their father's room.

What About YOU? **What do you think will happen? Check (✔) *Yes* or *No*.**

	Yes	No
1. Will Brendan and Anne be able to help?	_____	_____
2. Will Kevin go to San Francisco with Rebecca?	_____	_____
3. Will Kevin and Rebecca find the insurance papers?	_____	_____

Watch *PART 1.*

WHILE *You Watch*

7 **What does Brendan tell Rebecca? Check (✔) the sentences he says.**

1. _____ "A donation will do some good."

2. _____ "I feel so sorry for Kevin. Is he always this quiet?"

3. ___✔___ "It's hard to lose both parents when you're so young."

4. _____ "We should talk about how we can help."

5. _____ "No, but thanks for asking."

6. _____ "I'll call you in the morning."

AFTER *You Watch*

8 **How much do you remember about the story? Circle the answers.**

1. A neighbor brings flowers / food for Rebecca and Kevin.

2. Friends send money to Rebecca / the American Heart Association.

3. Kevin is / isn't usually a quiet person.

4. Rebecca says that Kevin likes / doesn't like to make plans.

5. Rebecca thanks Brendan and Anne for their help / money.

6. Brendan and Anne go back to the hotel / farm.

 **What do you think will happen? Check (✔) *I agree* or *I disagree*.**

	I agree	I disagree
1. Brendan and Anne will give money to Rebecca and Kevin.	_____	_____
2. Brendan and Anne will stay in Boston to help Rebecca and Kevin.	_____	_____

Watch PART 2.

WHILE You Watch

9 Who is speaking? Write **R** for *Rebecca*, or **K** for *Kevin*.

1. __R__ "This neighborhood sure is changing."

2. _____ "It just doesn't feel real yet."

3. _____ "First I'm going to become a millionaire."

4. _____ "I can't leave you here alone."

5. _____ "Let's get a pizza."

AFTER You Watch

10 How much do you remember about the story? Check (✔) *Yes* or *No*.

	Yes	No
1. Is Rebecca surprised about the neighborhood?	✔	
2. Does Kevin really think he's going to be rich?		
3. Does Rebecca want Kevin to be serious?		
4. Does Kevin want Rebecca to stay in Boston?		
5. Does Rebecca think Kevin can take care of himself?		

11 What does Rebecca say to Kevin? Use the words in the box to complete the sentences.

college	decide	✔education	family	rent

1. "We both have to _____ what we're going to do."

2. "Can you afford the _____ on the apartment?"

3. "Dad said he wanted you to go to _____."

4. "You have to get an ___education___ so that you can make a living."

5. "You're my brother. You're the only real _____ that I have right now."

 Watch PART **3.**

WHILE You Watch

12 **What does Kevin say? Circle the words you hear.**

1. "How much do the checks / bills add up to?"
2. "How much is in the bank / savings account?"
3. "He used to talk about his insurance / savings."
4. "These shirts / shoes must be 20 years old."
5. "Someday I'd like to go to / live in Ireland."

AFTER You Watch

13 **How much do you remember about the story? Circle the answers.**

1. Rebecca and Kevin talk in the living room / kitchen.
2. Rebecca adds up the bills / tickets they have to pay.
3. Their mother's / father's funeral cost $4,000.
4. Kevin / Rebecca asks about their father's insurance policy.
5. They look for the policy in their father's bedroom / office.
6. They find a small box / package.

14 **How does Rebecca feel? Complete the sentences. Choose the answers.**

1. _____ Rebecca is _____ about paying the bills.
   a. worried   **b.** angry   **c.** happy

2. _____ Rebecca is _____ about the insurance policy.
   a. upset   **b.** surprised   **c.** angry

3. _____ It makes Rebecca _____ to go in her father's room.
   a. happy   **b.** sad   **c.** confused

 **Do you have a place to keep things that are important to you?**

What do you keep there?

I keep _____ .

...papers   ...photos   ...money

CULTURE

In the United States and Canada, there are many types of insurance. For example, you can buy health, automobile, or life insurance. Health insurance helps pay doctor or hospital bills. Automobile insurance helps pay the costs of a car accident.

A life insurance policy pays money after a person dies. The money goes to friends or family members. When you buy life insurance, you decide who will get the money.

 **What About YOU?** Check (✔) your answers.

	Yes	No
1. Do you have insurance?	_____	_____

2. What kind of insurance is important to you?

_____ health   _____ car

_____ life   _____ home

EXPRESSIONS

 Match the underlined words from the story with their meanings.

a. tell us

b. your father's death

c. the result is

✔**d.** I finished school a short time ago.

e. earn the money to pay bills

1. _____ in the letter: "... your father's passing ... "

2. _____ in the letter: "... let us know ... "

3. ___d___ Kevin: "I just got out of school."

4. _____ Rebecca: "... make a living ... "

5. _____ Frank: "... you end up ... "

REVIEW AND DISCUSS

STORY SUMMARY

16 Use the words in the box to complete the story summary for Episode 30.

bedroom	bills	can	gets	go	help	insurance
✔ kitchen	letters	plans	talk	walk	worried	

Rebecca, Brendan, and Anne sit in the Caseys' _____kitchen_____. They _____
(1)   (2)
about the future, and Rebecca reads _____ from friends. Rebecca wants to
(3)
_____ back to school, but she is _____ about Kevin and about money.
(4)   (5)
Brendan and Anne want to _____. Later, Rebecca and Kevin _____ around
(6)   (7)
the neighborhood. Rebecca wants Kevin to make some _____. He _____
(8)   (9)
angry at her. He says he _____ take care of himself. At home, Rebecca adds up the
(10)
_____ they have to pay. Kevin thinks their father had an _____ policy, and
(11)   (12)
they look for it in his _____.
(13)

VIEWPOINTS

17 Watch the Reflections segment. What does Frank mean?
Check (✔) *True* or *False.*

> *It was a good service. Lots of nice speeches... Always said I wanted a big party.*

Frank Wells

	True	False
1. Frank is talking about Patrick's funeral.	_____	_____
2. Frank wants a quiet funeral when he dies.	_____	_____

What About YOU? What is your opinion? Check (✔) *I agree* or *I disagree.*

	I agree	I disagree
1. Patrick Casey had a good funeral.	_____	_____
2. It is a good idea for families and friends to be together after a funeral.	_____	_____

A BOX OF MEMORIES

PREVIEW **In this episode, Rebecca and Kevin visit a bank. They get some good news.**

My father had a safe deposit box here. I have the key.

Mr. Ferguson, Rebecca, and Kevin at the bank

I had no idea he kept all this.

Kevin and Rebecca at the bank

I'd like to cash in his insurance policy.

Kevin and Rebecca at home

BEFORE You Watch

1 **Look at the photos above. Use the words in the box to complete the sentences.**

✔ box	calls	key	policy	surprised

1. Rebecca and Kevin find the key to a safe deposit ___box___.

2. They take the _____ to the bank.

3. Rebecca is _____ at the things in the safe deposit box.

4. She and Kevin find papers, photographs, and an insurance _____.

5. Rebecca _____ the insurance company.

What do you think will happen? Check (✔) Yes or No.

	Yes	No
1. Will Rebecca and Kevin get money from the insurance company?	_____	_____
2. Will Rebecca and Kevin be able to pay the bills?	_____	_____

WATCH FOR MAIN IDEAS

 Watch *all* of EPISODE 31, "A Box of Memories"

WHILE You Watch

2 Who does Rebecca talk to? Check (✔) their names.

1. Kevin
✔

2. Mr. Ferguson
☐

3. Uncle Brendan
☐

4. an insurance agent
☐

5. Sandy
☐

AFTER You Watch

3 How much do you remember about the story? Put the photos in order from 1 to 6.

a. _____

b. _____

c. ___1___

d. _____

e. _____

f. _____

Go back, Rebecca.

a.

They said we'd probably get the money in two to three months.

b.

Dad had a safe deposit box?

c.

Dad did have an insurance policy!

d.

It's a joint account with Rebecca Casey.

e.

Are we rich, or what?

f.

4 **How do Kevin and Rebecca feel? Check (✔) *Yes* or *No*.**

	Yes	No
1. Is Rebecca surprised about the safe deposit box?	✔	
2. Is Rebecca happy to find the things in the box?		
3. Does Rebecca feel rich now?		
4. Does Kevin want Rebecca to go back to San Francisco?		
5. Does Kevin want to stay in Boston?		

5 **What do you know about Kevin? Check (✔) the sentences that *are not* true.**

1. _____ Kevin wants to start college.

2. _____ He wants to buy a motorcycle.

3. ✔ He tells Rebecca to stay in Boston.

4. _____ He wants to live in the apartment with friends.

5. _____ He wants Rebecca to listen to him.

6. _____ He wants Rebecca to take care of him.

What do you think will happen? Check (✔) *Yes* or *No*.

	Yes	No
1. Will Kevin share the apartment with his friends?		
2. Will Rebecca go back to San Francisco?		
3. Will Rebecca and Kevin share the money?		

WATCH FOR DETAILS

Watch PART 1.

WHILE You Watch

6 Listen to Mr. Ferguson. Check (✔) the sentences he says.

1. _____ "May I help you?"

2. _____ "What's the box number?"

3. _____ "Where is the key?"

4. ___✔___ "Is your name on the account?"

5. _____ "It's a joint account with Rebecca Casey."

6. _____ "Wait here. I'll be right back."

AFTER You Watch

7 How much do you remember about the story? Check (✔) *True* or *False*.

	True	False
1. The name of the bank is on the key.	✔	_____
2. Rebecca has the number of the safe deposit box.	_____	_____
3. Kevin's name is on the account.	_____	_____
4. The bank officer asks to see Rebecca's driver's license.	_____	_____
5. Rebecca and Kevin can look in the box at home.	_____	_____

8 What are Rebecca and Kevin thinking?
Complete the sentence. Check (✔) the answer.

Rebecca and Kevin _____
what is in the safe deposit box.

_____ **a.** know

_____ **b.** want to know

_____ **c.** don't care

Watch PART 2.

WHILE You Watch

9 **What does Rebecca say to Kevin? Circle the words you hear.**

1. "Look, it's a picture of Dad and Uncle Brendan / Mom."

2. "Grandma and Grandpa's passports from Ireland / France."

3. "It's an old, Irish necklace / ring."

4. "The hands mean money / friendship."

5. "No, I never saw this ring on Mom's / Dad's finger."

AFTER You Watch

10 **How much do you remember about the story? Complete the sentences. Choose the answers.**

1. _____a_____ Patrick kept a letter from _a woman he saved in a fire_.
   a. a woman he saved in a fire   **b.** his mother   **c.** Brendan

2. _____ There is a program from one of _____ music recitals.
   a. Rebecca's   **b.** Kevin's   **c.** Mrs. Casey's

3. _____ _____ came to the United States from Ireland in 1920.
   a. Patrick Casey   **b.** Patrick's parents   **c.** Margaret Casey

4. _____ Rebecca and Kevin think the ring belonged to _____.
   a. their grandmother   **b.** Aunt Molly   **c.** Uncle Brendan

5. _____ Rebecca and Kevin can get $4,000 from the _____.
   a. ring   **b.** savings bonds   **c.** insurance policy

11 **What do you know about Patrick Casey? Check (✔) Yes or No.**

	Yes	No
1. Did he care about his family?	_____	_____
2. Did he plan ahead for his children?	_____	_____
3. Did he talk to his children about his feelings?	_____	_____

Watch PART 3.

WHILE You Watch

12 **Who is speaking? Write R for _Rebecca,_ or K for _Kevin._**

1. __R__ "We're not rich."
2. _____ "So what are we going to do?"
3. _____ "Maybe we should talk to Uncle Brendan."
4. _____ "That's what Dad would want, too."
5. _____ "I can take care of myself."
6. _____ "Let me think about it."

AFTER You Watch

13 **How much do you remember about the story? Put the sentences in order from 1 to 5. Then write the sentences in the correct order below.**

a. _____ Kevin tells Rebecca he wants to share the apartment with friends.

b. _____ Rebecca calls the insurance company about the $50,000 policy.

c. ____1____ Kevin gets excited about spending the money.

d. _____ Rebecca tells Kevin that she wants to go back to San Francisco.

e. _____ Rebecca will think about Kevin's idea.

1. ___Kevin gets excited about spending the money.___

2. _____

3. _____

4. _____

5. _____

What is your opinion? Check (✔) _I agree_ or _I disagree._

	I agree	I disagree
1. Kevin can take care of himself.	_____	_____
2. Rebecca should go back to San Francisco.	_____	_____

HIGHLIGHTS

CULTURE

Many people from other countries come to the United States and Canada to live. They are called immigrants.

Millions of immigrants first entered the United States at Ellis Island. Today, it is a museum.

Ellis Island

Statue of Liberty

...to work ...to find a better life ...to be with their family

 **Why do people immigrate?**

People immigrate _____

_____ .

EXPRESSIONS

(14) **Match the underlined words from the story with their meanings. Check (✔) the answers.**

1. Kevin: "Are you kidding me?"
   _____ **a.** Are you asking me?
   ✔ **b.** Are you making a joke?

2. Operator: "Can you hold, please?"
   _____ **a.** Will you please wait?
   _____ **b.** Will you please call again later?

3. Rebecca: "It's not a big deal."
   _____ **a.** It's easy; it's no problem.
   _____ **b.** It's not expensive.

4. Kevin: "We're broke."
   _____ **a.** We're rich.
   _____ **b.** We have no money.

5. Kevin: "Let's get this out in the open."
   _____ **a.** I want to talk about this.
   _____ **b.** I want to stop talking about this.

REVIEW AND DISCUSS

STORY SUMMARY

15 **Use the words in the box to complete the story summary for Episode 31.**

bank	box	do	for	go	grandparents'	
insurance	✔keys	live	ring	savings	tells	think

Rebecca and Kevin find the _____keys_____ to a safe deposit _____. They
(1)   (2)

go to the _____ and open the box. They find letters, an Irish _____, their
(3)   (4)

_____ passports, photographs, _____ bonds, and a life _____
(5)   (6)   (7)

policy. They can cash in the insurance policy _____ $50,000. Rebecca and Kevin talk
(8)

about what they will _____. Kevin _____ Rebecca to _____
(9)   (10)   (11)

back to San Francisco. He wants some friends to _____ in the apartment with him.
(12)

Rebecca says she will _____ about this idea.
(13)

VIEWPOINTS

> I would use it for
> something fun.

16 **Watch the video discussion group. What does Yukiyoshi mean?
Check (✔) *True* or *False*.**

	True	False
1. Yukiyoshi is talking about the $50,000 insurance money.	_____	_____
2. If he got a lot of money, he would save it.	_____	_____

**Yukiyoshi Ozawa,
Japan**

What About YOU?

What would you do with $50,000? Check (✔) your answer.

1. _____ I would save it.

2. _____ I would spend it.

3. _____ I would give it away.

THE MISSING CAR

PREVIEW **In this episode, Rebecca and Kevin talk about their plans for the future. Brendan and Anne want to help them.**

We want you to have the ring.

Brendan, Anne, Rebecca, and Kevin at a restaurant

I'm not a child!

Kevin outside of the restaurant

Come home with us.

Rebecca, Brendan, and Anne at home

BEFORE You Watch

1 **Look at the photos above. Check (✔) *True* or *False*.**

	True	False
1. Rebecca and Kevin go to a restaurant with Brendan and Anne.	✔	
2. Rebecca tells them about the things in the safe deposit box.		
3. Kevin gets upset.		
4. Kevin wants Rebecca to make decisions for him.		
5. Brendan wants Rebecca and Kevin to move to San Francisco.		

2 **What does Kevin want? Complete the sentence. Check (✔) the answer.**

Kevin wants Rebecca to understand that he is _____.

_____ **a.** just a child   _____ **b.** now an adult

What About YOU? **When do people become adults?**

They are adults _____.

...when they start to work *...at age 21* *...when they get married*

WATCH FOR MAIN IDEAS

 Watch *all* of EPISODE 32, "The Missing Car."

WHILE You Watch

3 **Who does Rebecca talk to? Check (✔) their names.**

1. Brendan
☑

2. Kevin
☐

3. Anne
☐

4. Laura
☐

AFTER You Watch

4 **How much do you remember about the story? Put the sentences in order from 1 to 5. Then write the sentences in the correct order below.**

a. _____ Brendan talks about Rebecca and Kevin visiting the farm.

b. _____ Kevin gets angry at Rebecca and starts to walk home.

c. _____ In the apartment, Rebecca, Brendan, and Anne talk about the future.

d ___1___ Rebecca tells Brendan and Anne about the safe deposit box.

e. _____ Kevin takes Brendan's car.

1. _____Rebecca tells Brendan and Anne about the safe deposit box._____

2. _____

3. _____

4. _____

5. _____

5 **What do these people want? Check (✔) Yes or No.**

	Yes	No
1. Does Rebecca want Kevin to live with his friends?	_____	✔
2. Does Kevin want Rebecca to decide what he should do?	_____	_____
3. Does Brendan want Kevin to take the car?	_____	_____
4. Do Brendan and Anne want to help Rebecca and Kevin?	_____	_____
5. Do they want to give money to Rebecca and Kevin?	_____	_____

6 **Who is Laura? Complete the sentence. Check (✔) the answer.**

Laura is _____.

_____ **a.** the Caseys' neighbor   _____ **b.** Kevin's girlfriend   _____ **c.** Rebecca's friend

What About **YOU?** **What do you think will happen? Check (✔) Yes or No.**

	Yes	No
1. Will Brendan find out the car is gone?	_____	_____
2. Will Kevin come home safe?	_____	_____
3. Will Rebecca and Kevin go to the farm?	_____	_____

WATCH FOR DETAILS

 Watch PART 1.

WHILE You Watch

7 **What does Rebecca tell Brendan and Anne? Check (✔) the sentences she says.**

1. ___✔___ "The Union Oyster House is one of the oldest restaurants in the United States."
2. _____ "I'll take your coats."
3. _____ "By the way, this is my treat."
4. _____ "You'll love them."
5. _____ "We have some good news."
6. _____ "We found a metal box in Dad's room."

AFTER You Watch

8 **How much do you remember about the story? Check (✔) True or False.**

	True	False
1. The Union Oyster House is an old restaurant.	✔	
2. Everyone likes the oysters.		
3. Rebecca tells Brendan and Anne about the $50,000.		
4. Brendan is happy to have the ring.		
5. Brendan will wear the ring.		

9 **What do these people do? Circle the answers.**

1. Who wants to pay for dinner?   Rebecca / Kevin

2. Who shares their good news?   Brendan and Anne / Rebecca and Kevin

3. Who remembers his mother's ring?   Brendan / Kevin

 **Do you like to try new foods? Complete the sentence. Circle your answer.**

I _____ like to try new foods.

usually   sometimes   never

Watch PART 2.

WHILE You Watch

10 Who is speaking? Write **R** for *Rebecca*, **K** for *Kevin*, or **B** for *Brendan*.

1. __B__ "When are you returning to California and college?"
2. _____ "I never agreed to that."
3. _____ "Maybe I'll take the rest of the semester off."
4. _____ "Hey, leave me alone!"
5. _____ "It's not easy for a kid to lose his parents."
6. _____ "Why did I ever leave Boston in the first place?"

AFTER You Watch

11 How much do you remember about the story? Complete the sentences. Choose the answers.

a. return to college   d. Brendan's rental car
✔b. his friends   e. doesn't see
c. Rebecca   f. the restaurant

1. _____ Rebecca, Kevin, Brendan, and Anne leave _____.

2. _____ Anne thinks Rebecca should _____.

3. ___b___ Kevin wants to be with ___his friends___.

4. _____ Kevin gets upset with _____.

5. _____ Kevin takes _____.

6. _____ Rebecca _____ Kevin take the car.

12 Read what the Caseys say. How do they feel? Check (✔) the answers.

1. Anne says, "Oh, don't give up school."
   She is _____ **a.** angry _____ **b.** worried

2. Kevin says, "You do what you want, I'll do what I want!"
   He is _____ **a.** happy _____ **b.** angry

3. Brendan says, "There must be something we can do."
   He is _____ **a.** positive _____ **b.** negative

 Watch PART **3.**

WHILE You Watch

13 **What does Brendan say? Circle the words you hear.**

1. "I <u>can/don't</u> understand that."

2. "Do you think this is the <u>right/correct</u> time?"

3. "Anne and I have been <u>reading/talking</u> about this whole situation . . ."

4. "That would give you both <u>time/money</u> to think about what you want to do."

5. "You're our <u>family/friends</u>."

6. "Come home with us . . . even for a <u>weekend/short while</u>."

AFTER You Watch

14 **How much do you remember about the story? Circle the answers.**

1. Kevin goes to Laura's <u>house/college</u>.

2. Kevin and Laura <u>go for a ride/stay home</u>.

3. Rebecca says Kevin needs <u>time to think/a new job</u>.

4. Anne and Brendan tell their idea to <u>Rebecca/Kevin</u>.

5. Brendan and Anne want Kevin and Rebecca to <u>buy/visit</u> their farm.

6. At the farm, Rebecca and Kevin can meet their <u>grandmother/cousins</u>.

 **What is your opinion? Check (✔) Yes or No.**

	Yes	No
1. Does Brendan have a good idea for Rebecca and Kevin?	_____	_____
2. Does Rebecca like Brendan's idea?	_____	_____
3. Will Kevin like Brendan's idea?	_____	_____

CULTURE

In the United States and Canada, when people eat together in restaurants, they can choose to pay in different ways.

I'll take the check.

Sometimes one person pays for everyone.

Can we have separate checks, please?

Sometimes each person pays for himself or herself.

What About YOU? **Check (✔) Yes or No.**

	Yes	No
1. In your country, do people ever ask for separate checks?	_____	_____
2. Do you ever pay for everyone?	_____	_____

EXPRESSIONS

 15 Match the underlined words from the story with their meanings.

It's a very bad idea for you to quit school.

a.

1. _____ " This is my treat."

2. _____ " These are not for me."

3. _____ " This means a great deal to me."

4. ___a___ " It's crazy for you to drop out."

I don't like these.

b.

This is very important to me.

c.

I'll pay for this. TICKETS

NEW SHOW

d.

REVIEW AND DISCUSS

STORY SUMMARY

16 Use the words in the box to complete the story summary for Episode 32.

angry	apartment	car	care	farm	idea
listens	money	✔restaurant	see	them	things

Rebecca and Kevin go to a ___restaurant___ with Brendan and Anne. Rebecca tells
_____ (2) about the _____ (3) they found in the safe deposit box, and the

_____ (4) from the insurance policy. She gives Brendan the ring. They leave the restaurant,

and Rebecca talks about taking _____ (5) of Kevin. He gets _____ (6) and walks

away. At the _____ (7), Rebecca, Brendan, and Anne talk about Kevin. Kevin comes in,

_____ (8) to them, and runs out. He takes Brendan's _____ (9), and he goes to

_____ (10) Laura, his girlfriend. Brendan tells Rebecca his _____ (11). He wants

Rebecca and Kevin to visit the _____ (12).

VIEWPOINTS

> You make big mistakes on impulse.

Olga Baloueff, Belgium

17 Watch the video discussion group.
What does Olga mean? Circle the answers.

1. Olga thinks it was a <u>good/bad</u> idea for Kevin to take the car.

2. She thinks it is good to <u>plan our actions/act without thinking</u>.

What About YOU? What is your opinion? Check (✔) *I agree* or *I disagree*.

	I agree	I disagree
1. Nobody is listening to Kevin.	_____	_____
2. Kevin needs to make his own decisions.	_____	_____
3. Kevin needs to listen to someone older.	_____	_____

A BREAKDOWN

 **PREVIEW** In this episode, Kevin and Laura talk. Rebecca tries to find her brother. Everyone worries about him.

How come you didn't write me?

Laura and Kevin by Boston Harbor

Have you seen or heard from Kevin?

Rebecca and Sandy on the phone

Why did Dad have to die?

Kevin and Rebecca at the park

BEFORE You Watch

1 **Look at the photos above. Check (✔) Yes or No.**

	Yes	No
1. Is Kevin upset with Laura?	✔	
2. Did Laura write to Kevin?		
3. Does Rebecca call Sandy about Kevin?		
4. Does Rebecca find Kevin?		
5. Does Kevin need his father?		

 **What is your opinion? Check (✔) Yes or No.**

	Yes	No
1. People feel better if they talk about their feelings.		
2. It is a good idea to talk to family members about your feelings.		

Watch *all* of EPISODE 33, "A Breakdown."

WHILE You Watch

 What does Kevin say? Circle the words you hear.

1. "I'm not angry/sad."

2. "How long does it take to write/send a letter?"

3. "When are you going back to school/work?"

4. "I took your car/money."

5. "Just leave me/them alone!"

6. "I've done enough talking/driving for one night."

AFTER You Watch

 How much do you remember about the story? Put the photos in order from 1 to 5.

a. _____

b. ___1___

c. _____

d. _____

e. _____

a. *That was not a clever thing to do.*

b. *I'm just not ready to get serious with anyone.*

c. *I know it hurts.*

d. *Where's my car?*

e. *Poor kid. …No, I haven't seen him.*

4 **Use the words in the box to complete the sentences.**

| adult | ask | car | father | look | sorry |

1. Laura feels _____ for Kevin.

2. Rebecca, Brendan, and Anne _____ for the car keys.

3. Rebecca calls Sandy to _____ about Kevin.

4. Rebecca gets angry at Kevin about the _____.

5. Kevin is not acting like an _____adult_____.

6. Kevin misses his _____.

5 **How does Kevin feel? Check (✔) the sentences that *are not* true.**

_____ **a.** Kevin is unhappy about Laura's new friends.

_____ **b.** He is sad that his father died.

___✔___ **c.** He doesn't care about the insurance money.

_____ **d.** He is worried about his future.

_____ **e.** He is angry at Sandy.

 **What do you think will happen? Check (✔) Yes or No.**

	Yes	No
1. Will Brendan forgive Kevin for taking the car?	_____	_____
2. Will Laura write to Kevin?	_____	_____

WATCH FOR DETAILS

 Watch PART 1.

WHILE You Watch

6 Who is speaking? Write K for *Kevin,* L for *Laura,* or B for *Brendan.*

1. __K__ "It's my favorite spot."

2. _____ "What are you going to do?"

3. _____ "The airport's really busy tonight."

4. _____ "I knew you'd understand."

5. _____ "Are you going to be OK?"

6. _____ "When are you going back to school?"

AFTER You Watch

7 How much do you remember about the story? Circle the answers.

1. Kevin and Laura go to (Kevin's)/Laura's favorite place.

2. Laura / Kevin talks about college.

3. Kevin / Laura has new friends now.

4. Brendan / Rebecca is going back to the hotel.

5. Rebecca finds out about the missing car / Kevin's visit to Laura.

6. Kevin and Laura say goodbye / make plans for the future.

8 How do Kevin and Laura feel? Check (✔) *Yes* or *No.*

	Yes	No
1. Does Kevin like Laura?	_____	_____
2. Does Kevin want Laura to write to him?	_____	_____
3. Does Laura want Kevin to be her boyfriend?	_____	_____

 Watch PART 2.

WHILE You Watch

9 Who is angry? Circle the answers.

1. (Jack)   2. Sandy   3. Rebecca   4. Brendan   5. Kevin

AFTER You Watch

10 How much do you remember about the story? Put the sentences in order from 1 to 5. Then write the sentences in the correct order below.

a. _____ Kevin comes back.

b. _____ Jack pulls the phone off the wall.

c. _____ Kevin runs out of the apartment.

d. _____ Rebecca yells at Kevin.

e. ____1____ Rebecca calls Sandy.

1. _____ Rebecca calls Sandy. _____

2. _____

3. _____

4. _____

5. _____

11 What do you know about these people? Circle the answers.

1. Who looks very bad?   Rebecca (Sandy)

2. Who feels sorry for Kevin?   Rebecca / Sandy

3. Who is dangerous?   Jack / Kevin

4. Who is angry about the car?   Brendan / Jack

5. Who wants Kevin to say he is sorry?   Rebecca / Anne

 What About YOU? What is your opinion? Check (✔) Yes or No.

	Yes	No
1. Do you feel sorry for Kevin?	_____	_____
2. Are you worried about Sandy?	_____	_____

Watch PART 3.

WHILE You Watch

 12 **What does Rebecca tell Kevin? Check (✔) the sentences she says.**

1. _____ "Kevin, stop acting like a child!"
2. _____ "I know you're mad at me."
3. ___✔___ "When I was driving to California by myself, I felt pretty bad."
4. _____ "I really love this song."
5. _____ "But we've got some decisions to make."
6. _____ "Uncle Brendan came up with an idea."

AFTER You Watch

 13 **How much do you remember about the story? Check (✔) True or False.**

	True	False
1. Brendan follows Kevin to the park.	_____	✔
2. Rebecca stops being angry at Kevin.	_____	_____
3. Kevin cries in the park.	_____	_____
4. Kevin talks to Rebecca about Laura.	_____	_____
5. Rebecca sings to Kevin.	_____	_____
6. Rebecca and Kevin leave the park together.	_____	_____

14 **How does Kevin feel? Circle the answers.**

1. He wants / doesn't want to make his own decisions.

2. Rebecca's song makes him feel better / worse.

 **What is your opinion? Check (✔) I agree or I disagree.**

	I agree	I disagree
1. Rebecca understands Kevin's feelings.	_____	_____
2. Kevin needs to listen to Rebecca.	_____	_____
3. Rebecca needs to listen to Kevin.	_____	_____

CULTURE

In the United States and Canada, men do not usually cry in public places. They do not like to show sad feelings.

 **Check (✔) Yes or No.**

	Yes	No
1. In your country, do men show sad feelings?	_____	_____
2. Do you think it is OK for men to cry?	_____	_____

EXPRESSIONS

 Match the underlined words from the story with their meanings.

✔ **a.** It might not work.
  b. busy with
  c. difficult
  d. very interested in it
  e. spends time with

1. _____ Laura: "It must be <u>tough</u>."

2. _____ Laura: "The professors and students are <u>really into it</u>."

3. _____ Laura: "I've been <u>all wrapped up in</u> school."

4. ____a____ Rebecca: "<u>This is a long shot</u>."

5. _____ Rebecca: "Do you know who he <u>hangs around with</u> these days?"

STORY SUMMARY

16 **Use the words in the box to complete the story summary for Episode 33.**

angry	calls	car	comes	feels	find	follows
girlfriend		park	phone		sings	✔ write

Kevin and Laura talk. He is upset. Laura didn't _____write_____ to him from college. She (1)

_____ sorry for Kevin, but she doesn't want to be his _____. Rebecca finds (2) (3)

out about the missing _____. She _____ Kevin's friends. She wants to (4) (5)

_____ him. Her call to Sandy makes Jack _____, and he pulls the (6) (7)

_____ off the wall. Kevin _____ back. Rebecca and Brendan get angry at (8) (9)

him. Kevin runs out and Rebecca _____ him. She finds him in a _____. He is (10) (11)

crying. Now she feels sorry for Kevin. She _____ him a funny song. They talk, and then (12)

they leave together.

VIEWPOINTS

Most of the time, they are not really friends.

17 **Watch the video discussion group. What does Patrick mean? Complete the sentences. Choose the answers.**

1. _____ Patrick is talking about _____.

   a. brothers **b.** Rebecca **c.** Sandy
   and sisters and Kevin and Jack

2. _____ He thinks brothers and sisters are _____ friends.

   a. always **b.** never **c.** not usually

Patrick Jerome, Haiti

What About YOU? **What is your opinion? Check (✔) *I agree* or *I disagree*.**

	I agree	I disagree
1. Rebecca and Kevin are friends.	_____	_____
2. Brothers and sisters are usually friends.	_____	_____

A CALL FOR HELP

PREVIEW In this episode, Brendan tells Kevin his idea. Sandy makes an important decision.

It would give you some time to think things over.

Kevin, Rebecca, Brendan, and Anne at breakfast

I've got to get out of here quick.

Sandy at home

Sandy, it's me, Rebecca.

Rebecca and Kevin at Sandy and Jack's apartment

BEFORE You Watch

1 Look at the photos above. Complete the sentences. Choose the answers.

1. _____ Brendan talks to _____ about visiting the farm.

   a. Rebecca **b.** Kevin **c.** Rebecca and Kevin

2. ____b____ Sandy is ____afraid of____ Jack.

   a. happy with **b.** afraid of **c.** married to

3. _____ Sandy decides to _____ Jack.

   a. leave **b.** stay with **c.** marry

4. _____ Sandy _____ Rebecca about her decision.

   a. goes to see **b.** calls **c.** writes to

5. _____ Rebecca goes to _____ to help Sandy.

   a. Sandy's apartment **b.** the police **c.** the hospital

What About YOU? What is your opinion? Check (✔) *I agree* or *I disagree*.

	I agree	I disagree
1. Rebecca shouldn't help Sandy.	_____	_____
2. Jack is a bad person.	_____	_____

WATCH FOR MAIN IDEAS

Watch *all* of EPISODE 34, "A Call for Help."

WHILE You Watch

2 **Who knows that Sandy is leaving? Check (✔) their names.**

1. Rebecca
✔

2. Kevin
☐

3. Jack
☐

4. the police
☐

5. Brendan
☐

AFTER You Watch

3 **How much do you remember about the story? Put the photos in order from 1 to 6.**

a. _____   **c.** _____   **e.** _____

b. _____   **d.** _____   **f.** ___1___

Our proposal is for you to come to Illinois…

a.

We'll be right over to pick you up.

b.

Let's get out of here…

c.

I'm moving out.

d.

I've made up my mind.

e.

I'm very sorry…

f.

4 How will Rebecca help Sandy? Check (✔) the answer.

_____ **a.** Rebecca will help Sandy move out of the apartment.

_____ **b.** Rebecca will go to the police.

_____ **c.** Rebecca will talk to Jack.

5 What do you know about these people? Complete the sentences with the phrases below.

a. is in trouble

b. is dangerous

c. needs to make a decision about the farm

d. wants Sandy to leave Jack

✔ **e.** takes Rebecca to get Sandy

1. _____ Rebecca _____.

2. _____ Kevin _____.

3. ____e____ Brendan _____takes Rebecca to get Sandy_____.

4. _____ Sandy _____.

5. _____ Jack _____.

6 What are Kevin's choices? Check (✔) the sentence that *is not* true.

_____ **a.** Kevin can go to San Francisco with Rebecca.

_____ **b.** He can go to the farm in Illinois.

_____ **c.** He can stay in Boston with Rebecca.

_____ **d.** He can stay in Boston alone.

What About **YOU?** What do you think will happen? Check (✔) *Yes* or *No*.

	Yes	No
1. Will Kevin go to the farm?	_____	_____
2. Will Sandy stay in the Caseys' apartment?	_____	_____
3. Will Sandy be safe from Jack?	_____	_____

WATCH FOR DETAILS

 Watch PART 1.

WHILE You Watch

7 Who is speaking? Write **K** for *Kevin*, **R** for *Rebecca*, or **A** for *Anne*.

1. __K__ "I apologize."
2. _____ "It's just that we were worried."
3. _____ "You don't have to ask me, honey."
4. _____ "But I have a job."
5. _____ "I'll do whatever you want."
6. _____ "Can we keep the apartment?"

AFTER You Watch

8 How much do you remember about the story? Check (✔) *True* or *False*.

	True	False
1. Kevin tells Brendan and Anne he is sorry.	✔	
2. Brendan and Anne come for breakfast.		
3. Anne tells Kevin about Brendan's idea.		
4. Kevin can choose what he wants to do.		
5. Kevin says he won't go to the farm.		
6. Rebecca and Kevin will keep the apartment.		

9 What do you know about these people? Check (✔) *Yes* or *No*.

	Yes	No
1. Do Brendan and Anne forgive Kevin?	✔	
2. Is Kevin surprised about Brendan's idea?		
3. Will Rebecca do what Kevin wants?		
4. Is Kevin angry at Rebecca?		
5. Will Kevin think about the plan?		

What About **YOU?** What is your opinion? Check (✔) *True* or *False*.

	True	False
1. Kevin isn't really sorry about taking the car.		
2. Kevin should do what Rebecca wants him to do.		

Watch PART 2.

WHILE You Watch

 10 **Listen to Rebecca. Check (✔) the sentences she says.**

1. _____ "What happened last night?"

2. _____ "What did Jack do?"

3. _____ "Yes, he's home and he's fine."

4. ___✔___ "Good for you."

5. _____ "You can stay at my mother's."

6. _____ "I don't want to hear another word."

AFTER You Watch

11 **How much do you remember about the story? Use the words in the box to complete the sentences.**

leave	✔ pick up	problem	stay	tells

1. Sandy _____ Rebecca about her decision.

2. Sandy plans to _____ Jack.

3. She can _____ at Rebecca's apartment.

4. Rebecca will ____*pick up*____ Sandy right away.

5. Rebecca tells Kevin, Brendan, and Anne about Sandy's _____.

12 **How do Sandy and Rebecca feel? Complete the sentences with the words below.**

a. happy   **d.** scared

✔**b.** worried   **e.** to move out

c. to help

1. ___b___ Rebecca was ___*worried*___ about Sandy.

2. _____ Sandy wants _____ of Jack's apartment.

3. _____ Sandy's decision makes Rebecca _____.

4. _____ Sandy feels _____.

5. _____ Rebecca wants _____ Sandy.

 Watch PART 3.

WHILE You Watch

13 **What does Sandy say? Circle the words you hear.**

1. "Jack, there's something I want to <u>tell</u>/<u>show</u> you."
2. "I'm <u>moving</u>/<u>going</u> out."
3. "I <u>think</u>/<u>know</u> you heard me."
4. "He's (gone)/ <u>sick</u> ."
5. "There, I packed my <u>stuff</u> / <u>suitcase</u>. Let's go."

AFTER You Watch

14 **How much do you remember about the story? Put the sentences in order from 1 to 5. Then write the sentences in the correct order below.**

a. _____ Jack goes out.

b. _____ Rebecca and Kevin help Sandy finish packing.

c. _____ Jack gets angry and hits Sandy.

d. ___1___ Sandy tells Jack that she is moving out.

e. _____ Sandy runs into the bathroom.

1. _____ Sandy tells Jack that she is moving out. _____

2. _____

3. _____

4. _____

5. _____

6. _____

What About YOU? **What is your opinion? Check (✔) I agree or I disagree.**

	I agree	I disagree
1. Sandy needs to tell the police about Jack.	_____	_____
2. Sandy should try to be friends with Jack.	_____	_____

CULTURE

"Domestic violence" means violence in the home. In the United States and Canada, many people are hurt in their own homes. Most of the people who get hurt are women and children.

Domestic violence can happen in all kinds of families. It can happen in rich families and poor families.

 **What About YOU?** Check (✔) Yes or No.

	Yes	No
1. Do people in your country talk about domestic violence?	_____	_____
2. Can we protect people from this violence?	_____	_____

EXPRESSIONS

15 **Match the underlined words from the story with their meanings. Choose the answers.**

1. ___a___ Brendan: "It's over."

   a. It's finished.   **b.** It's still happening.

2. _____ Sandy: "I've made up my mind."

   a. I made a decision.   **b.** I made a mistake.

3. _____ Sandy: "I've had it!"

   a. I will try again.   **b.** I will not continue.

4. _____ Sandy: "I am leaving . . . for good."

   a. I am going and not coming back.   **b.** I am going for only a short time.

5. _____ Rebecca: "We'll be right over."

   a. We will wait here.   **b.** We are coming now.

REVIEW AND DISCUSS

STORY SUMMARY

16 Use the words in the box to complete the story summary for Episode 34.

angry	apartment	eat	finishes	✔ goes	hits
idea	leaving	pick up	sorry	tells	think

Kevin _____**goes**_____ home with Rebecca. He tells Brendan and Anne he is
(1)

_____. The next morning they _____ breakfast together. Brendan
(2) (3)

tells Kevin his _____ about the farm. Kevin wants to _____ about it.
(4) (5)

Sandy calls to say that she is _____ Jack. Rebecca tells Sandy she can stay in
(6)

the Caseys' _____. Rebecca says she will go _____ Sandy right away. Sandy
(7) (8)

_____ Jack she is leaving, and he _____ her. She goes into the bathroom,
(9) (10)

and Jack leaves. He is very _____. Rebecca and Kevin get to the apartment. Sandy
(11)

_____ packing, and they leave.
(12)

VIEWPOINTS

17 Watch the video discussion group. What does Patrick mean?
Check (✔) *True* or *False*.

> She always expects he will change.

Patrick Jerome,
Haiti

	True	False
1. Patrick is talking about Rebecca and Kevin.	_____	_____
2. Patrick thinks Sandy loves Jack.	_____	_____

What About YOU? What is your opinion? Check (✔) *I agree* or *I disagree*.

	I agree	I disagree
1. Jack has more than one problem.	_____	_____
2. People like Jack can change.	_____	_____

CHANGES

PREVIEW In this episode, Jack tries to make Sandy stay with him. Kevin makes a decision about his future.

Get out of my way.

Sandy and Jack at
the apartment building

Sandy! I've been waiting to hear from you. Are you OK?

Kevin and Rebecca
in their living room

It's strange to think someone else will be living here.

Kevin and Rebecca at home

BEFORE You Watch

(1) **Look at the photos above. Check (✔) *Yes* or *No*.**

	Yes	No
1. Does Jack want to stop Sandy?	✔	
2. Does Sandy want to stay with Jack?		
3. Does Sandy call Rebecca?		
4. Is Rebecca worried about Sandy?		
5. Are Rebecca and Kevin leaving Boston?		

(2) **What do you know about Jack? Check (✔) the sentence that *is not* true.**

1. _____ Jack is violent. He hurts Sandy.

2. _____ Jack wants Sandy to stay with him.

3. _____ Jack wants to help Sandy.

What About YOU? **What is your opinion? Check (✔) *I agree* or *I disagree*.**

	I agree	I disagree
1. It is good for Sandy to leave Jack.		
2. Sandy needs help from the police.		

WATCH FOR MAIN IDEAS

 Watch *all* of EPISODE 35, "Changes."

WHILE You Watch

3 **Where does Sandy go? Check (✔) all the answers.**

1. her apartment
☑

2. the police station
☐

3. a women's shelter
☐

4. Rebecca's apartment
☐

5. a restaurant
☐

AFTER You Watch

4 **How much do you remember about the story? Put the sentences in order from 1 to 5. Then write the sentences in the correct order below.**

a. _____ Rebecca and Kevin leave.

b. _____ Rebecca and Sandy say goodbye.

c. _____ Sandy goes to a battered women's shelter.

d. _____ Kevin decides to visit the farm.

e. ___1___ Sandy calls the police, and they arrest Jack.

1. _____ Sandy calls the police, and they arrest Jack. _____

2. _____

3. _____

4. _____

5. _____

How does Sandy feel? Check (✔) *True* or *False*.

	True	False
1. Sandy feels very happy now.	_____	✔
2. She is afraid of the police.	_____	_____
3. She wants to see Jack.	_____	_____
4. She feels bad about her problem.	_____	_____
5. She is glad to get help at the shelter.	_____	_____
6. She will miss Rebecca.	_____	_____

 What do you know about Rebecca and Kevin? Circle the answers.

1. Rebecca is happy / upset that Sandy calls the police.

2. Rebecca and Kevin are angry at / worried about Sandy.

3. Kevin wants to visit the farm / San Francisco.

4. Rebecca is sorry / happy about Kevin's decision.

5. Rebecca and Kevin are sad / excited to leave the apartment.

6. Rebecca wants / doesn't want to go see Sandy.

 **What do you think will happen? Check (✔) *Yes* or *No*.**

	Yes	No
1. Will Kevin like the farm?	_____	_____
2. Will Rebecca stay at the farm with Kevin?	_____	_____
3. Will Sandy have any more problems with Jack?	_____	_____

WATCH FOR DETAILS

Watch PART 1.

WHILE You Watch

7 Who is speaking? Write **R** for *Rebecca,* **S** for *Sandy,* or **J** for *Jack.*

1. __R__ "Let her go, Jack!"
2. _____ "You lay a hand on me and I'll see you in court!"
3. _____ "You're going to pay for this!"
4. _____ "They don't want anybody to know the location."
5. _____ "I'll call in a couple of days or so."

AFTER You Watch

8 **How much do you remember about the story? Put the photos in order from 1 to 5.**

a. _____

b. _____

c. ___1___

d. _____

e. _____

Is this the women's shelter?

a.

Are you all right?

b.

Sandy, go call the police.

c.

d.

My boyfriend hit me.

e.

9 **What do you know about these people? Circle the answers.**

1. Who is angry?	(Jack) / Sandy
2. Who wants to stop Sandy?	Kevin / Jack
3. Who yells at Jack?	Rebecca / Brendan
4. Who gets information from the police?	Rebecca / Sandy
5. Who needs to stay at the shelter?	Sandy / Jack

 Watch PART 2.

WHILE You Watch

10 **What does Kevin say? Circle the words you hear.**

1. "Maybe I'll go out to the farm for a while / year."
2. "Well, I need a change / vacation."
3. "Maybe I should check the mail / time."
4. "Would you like to talk to Rebecca / come over?"

AFTER You Watch

11 **How much do you remember about the story? Use the words in the box to complete the sentences.**

apartment	letter	picture	plans	✔ visit

1 Kevin decides to _____visit_____ the farm.

2. Rebecca and Kevin clean the _____ and pack their things.

3. Rebecca gets a _____ from Alex.

4. She reads the _____ from Ramón.

5. Rebecca and Sandy make _____ to meet.

12 **Look at the words in the box. Find and circle them in the puzzle.**

change	letter	mail	packing	✔ phone	picture

```
L  U  Q  M  R  Y  P  S
E  P  I  C  T  U  R  E
T  V  M  I  X  Z  C  H
T  K  A  L  J  D  H  P
E  W  I  F  S  B  A  L
R  U  L  P  H  O  N  E
P  A  C  K  I  N  G  A
W  Q  U  C  Z  X  E  O
```

What About YOU? **What is your opinion? Check (✔) Yes or No.**

	Yes	No
1. Is it fun to visit a farm?	_____	_____
2. Is a farm a good place to live?	_____	_____

Watch PART 3.

WHILE You Watch

13 **What does Rebecca tell Sandy? Check (✔) the sentences she says.**

1. ___✔___ "I was worried about you."
2. _____ "You're going for therapy?"
3. _____ "I'll miss you."
4. _____ "I'll write letters to you."
5. _____ "Here are the keys."

AFTER You Watch

14 **How much do you remember about the story? Complete the sentences with *Rebecca*, *Sandy*, or *Rebecca and Sandy*.**

1. __Rebecca and Sandy__ meet at the restaurant.
2. _____ is living at a shelter.
3. _____ will stay in Rebecca and Kevin's apartment.
4. _____ say goodbye.
5. _____ is sad about leaving.

15 **What do you know about Rebecca and Sandy? Complete the sentences with the words below.**

a. help   d. change
✔ b. future   e. her friend
c. difficult

1. _____ Sandy wants to _____ her life.
2. _____ The changes will be _____.
3. _____ Women at the shelter _____ Sandy.
4. _____ Rebecca will miss _____.
5. ___b___ Rebecca and Sandy hope for good things in the _____future_____.

What About YOU? **What is your opinion? Check (✔) *I agree* or *I disagree*.**

	I agree	I disagree
1. It's important to help people when they have problems.	_____	_____
2. People need to solve their own problems.	_____	_____

CULTURE

In the United States and Canada, there are many support groups. These are groups of people that share the same problem. For example, there are support groups for people who want to stop smoking and for people who want to lose weight.

People join support groups for information, advice, and friendship.

 **What About YOU?** Check (✔) *Yes* or *No*.

	Yes	No
1. In your country, do people join support groups?	_____	_____
2. When you have problems, do you talk to friends?	_____	_____

EXPRESSIONS

16 **Match the underlined words from the story with their meanings. Check (✔) the answers.**

1.

You're trying to sneak out on me.

_____ **a.** You're trying to leave without telling me.

_____ **b.** You're trying to scare me.

2.

Do you want to come over?

_____ **a.** Do you want to talk?

_____ **b.** Do you want to visit us?

3.

I'm not the only one in this mess.

_____ **a.** Other women have this problem too.

_____ **b.** Other women are angry too.

STORY SUMMARY

17 **Use the words in the box to complete the story summary for Episode 35.**

get	go	✔ leaves	letter	police	restaurant
tell	things	tries	visit	wants	

Sandy ____leaves____ the apartment building with Rebecca and Kevin. They meet Jack and
(1)

he _____ to stop Sandy. She calls the _____, and they come to arrest Jack.
(2)   (3)

They tell Sandy to _____ to court. She can _____ a restraining order
(4)   (5)

against Jack. The police _____ Sandy about a battered women's shelter. She goes to stay
(6)

there so that she will be safe. Kevin decides to _____ the farm, so he and Rebecca pack
(7)

their _____. Rebecca gets a _____ from Ramón with a picture from Alex.
(8)   (9)

She meets Sandy in a _____, and they say goodbye. Sandy _____ to change
(10)   (11)

her life. Rebecca and Kevin leave.

VIEWPOINTS

She realized you really make your own luck.

18 **Watch the video discussion group. What does Laura mean? Circle the answers.**

1. Laura is talking about <u>Sandy / Rebecca</u>.

2. She thinks Sandy's problems <u>were / were not</u> because of bad luck.

**Laura Eastment,
Argentina**

 What About YOU?   **What is your opinion? Check (✔) *I agree* or *I disagree*.**

	I agree	I disagree
1. Good people usually have good luck.	_____	_____
2. Bad people usually have bad luck.	_____	_____

THE FARM

PREVIEW In this episode, Rebecca and Kevin arrive at the farm. They make some plans for their future.

Welcome! So nice to see you!

Anne, Kevin, Rebecca, and Brendan at the farm

It's a struggle to run a small family farm.

Brendan and Kevin at the computer

I can help you out on the farm.

Brendan and Kevin in the barn

BEFORE You Watch

1 Look at the photos above. Use the words in the box to complete the sentences.

✔ computer	farm	hard	uncle	works

1. Anne is waiting for Rebecca and Kevin at the _____.

2. Kevin is interested in Brendan's ___computer_____.

3. Brendan says it is _____ to run a farm.

4. Kevin _____ with Brendan in the barn.

5. Kevin wants to help his _____.

**What About YOU?** How do you feel about computers? Check (✔) *True* or *False*.

	True	False
1. I am interested in computers.	_____	_____
2. I don't like computers.	_____	_____
3. Computers are fun.	_____	_____

WATCH FOR MAIN IDEAS

 Watch *all* of EPISODE 36, "The Farm."

WHILE You Watch

2 **What do you see on the farm? Check (✔) all the answers.**

1. the house
✔

2. the barn
☐

3. chickens
☐

4. cows
☐

AFTER You Watch

3 **How much do you remember about the story? Put the sentences in order from 1 to 5. Then write the sentences in the correct order below.**

a. _____ Brendan shows Rebecca and Kevin the barn and the cows.

b. _____ Kevin asks questions about the farm.

c. ___1___ Rebecca and Kevin arrive at the farm.

d. _____ Kevin talks to Rebecca in her room.

e. _____ Kevin wants to stay on the farm and help his uncle.

1. _____Rebecca and Kevin arrive at the farm._____

2. _____

3. _____

4. _____

5. _____

4 Read what the Caseys say. How do they feel? Complete the sentences. Check (✔) the answers.

1. Anne says, "It's so good to have you here."

   She is _____.

   _____ **a.** sad   _____ **b.** happy

2. Kevin says, "Can you actually make money farming?"

   He is _____.

   _____ **a.** interested   _____ **b.** bored

3. Rebecca says, "You and Uncle Brendan were at that computer half the night."

   She is ___happy___.

   ___✔___ **a.** happy   _____ **b.** sad

4. Brendan says, "It hasn't been a great year, but wait until the next."

   He is _____.

   _____ **a.** negative   _____ **b.** positive

5 Who is Michael? Check (✔) the answer.

_____ **a.** He is Anne's brother.

_____ **b.** He is Brendan and Anne's son.

_____ **c.** He is Brendan and Anne's grandson.

What About **YOU?**   What do you think will happen? Check (✔) *Yes* or *No*.

	Yes	No
1. Will Anne be glad that Kevin is staying?	_____	_____
2. Will Rebecca want to leave her family?	_____	_____
3. Will Rebecca be happy in San Francisco?	_____	_____

WATCH FOR DETAILS

 Watch PART 1.

WHILE You Watch

 6 **What does Anne say? Circle the words you hear.**

1. "Any flavor you want, as long as it's chocolate /(vanilla)."
2. "Here, I have some letters /messages for you."
3. "Rebecca, let me show you your room /some pictures."
4. "He and his wife live in town /on a farm."
5. "They are eager to meet their Boston cousins /you and Kevin."

AFTER You Watch

 7 **How much do you remember about the story? Complete the sentences with the phrases below. Choose the answers.**

    a. doesn't live on the farm   **d.** are Michael's daughters

    b. is happy to see Rebecca and Kevin   **e.** have a son, Michael

✔**c.** bought the farm many years ago   **f.** are coming to the farm for Thanksgiving

1. _____ Anne _____.
2. ___c___ Anne's family _____ bought the farm many years ago _____.
3. _____ Brendan and Anne _____.
4. _____ Michael _____.
5. _____ Katie and Erin _____.
6. _____ Michael and his family _____.

8 **What makes Rebecca sad? Complete the sentence. Check (✔) the answer.**

Rebecca is sad when she thinks about _____.

_____ **a.** her cousin Michael   _____ **b.** her father   _____ **c.** Kevin

What About YOU? **What is your opinion? Check (✔) I agree or I disagree.**

	I agree	I disagree
1. Rebecca is glad to be at the farm.	_____	_____
2. Brendan and Anne are good people.	_____	_____

Watch PART 2.

WHILE You Watch

9 Who does Kevin talk to? Check (✔) all the answers.

1. Brendan
☐

2. Rebecca
☐

3. Anne
☐

AFTER You Watch

10 How much do you remember about the story? Put the photos in order from 1 to 5.

a. _____

b. _____

c. _____

d. ___1___

e. _____

Can you actually make money farming?

a.

Maybe there is something we could do.

b.

Can I come in?

c.

We have 120 cows here.

d.

This year we're in trouble.

e.

11 What do you know about Brendan and Kevin? Check (✔) *Yes* or *No*.

	Yes	No
1. Does Kevin know a lot about farms?	_____	✔
2. Is Kevin interested in computers?	_____	_____
3. Is Brendan worried about money this year?	_____	_____
4. Does Kevin want to help his uncle?	_____	_____

Watch PART 3.

WHILE You Watch

12 Who is speaking? Write **A** for Anne, **K** for Kevin, or **B** for Brendan.

1. __A__ "How did you sleep, hon?"
2. _____ "Could you check the turkey?"
3. _____ "You've got to be high tech in today's world."
4. _____ "My job is a dead end."
5. _____ "We've got company coming."

AFTER You Watch

13 How much do you remember about the story? Check (✔) *True* or *False*.

	True	False
1. Rebecca helps Anne with Thanksgiving dinner.	✔	
2. Kevin helps Brendan in the barn.		
3. Michael and his family are coming today.		
4. Brendan asks Kevin to stay and work on the farm.		
5. Kevin will pay rent to Brendan and Anne.		

14 What do you know about these people? Circle the answers.

1. Who doesn't like the smell in the barn?   Brendan /(Kevin)
2. Who teaches a computer course?   Brendan /Michael
3. Who thinks Rebecca worries too much?   Brendan /Kevin
4. Who wants to change his life?   Brendan /Kevin
5. Who wants to give Brendan and Anne money?   Rebecca /Kevin

 **What is your opinion? Check (✔) *Yes* or *No*.**

	Yes	No
1. Is it a good idea for Kevin to change his life?		
2. Can Kevin learn a lot from Brendan and Anne?		

CULTURE

In the United States and Canada, many farms are now big businesses. There are not many small family farms. It is hard to make a living on a small farm.

 **What About YOU?** Check (✔) *Yes* or *No*.

	Yes	No
1. Are there many farms in your country?	_____	_____
2. Are the farms usually family farms?	_____	_____
3. Do farmers make a lot of money?	_____	_____

EXPRESSIONS

 15 Match the underlined words from the story with their meanings.

    a. We're finished.

✔**b.** I disagree.

    c. Oh yes, of course.

    d. You have changed your decision.

    e. We aren't working anymore today.

1. _____ " <u>Oh, you bet</u> ."

2. _____ " <u>That's it</u> ."

3. _____ " <u>We're taking the rest of the day off</u> ."

4. _____ " <u>It's quite a change of heart</u> ."

5. ___b___ " <u>I wouldn't say that</u> ."

REVIEW AND DISCUSS

STORY SUMMARY

16 **Use the words in the box to complete the story summary for Episode 36.**

✔arrive	bad	barn	college	computer	cows	day
happy	hard	help	kitchen	stay	takes	

Rebecca and Kevin _____arrive_____ at the farm. Anne is _____ to see them.
(1)   (2)

Brendan _____ Rebecca and Kevin to the barn and shows them the _____.
(3)   (4)

In the house, he shows Kevin his _____. This is a _____ year for the farm.
(5)   (6)

It is _____ to make money on a small family farm. Kevin talks with Rebecca. He wants
(7)

to _____ his uncle. The next _____ is Thanksgiving. Rebecca helps Anne in
(8)   (9)

the _____, and Kevin works with Brendan in the _____. Kevin says he
(10)   (11)

wants to _____ on the farm. Then Rebecca can go back to _____. Brendan
(12)   (13)

likes this plan.

> He has high tech in the middle of the country.

VIEWPOINTS

17 **Watch the video discussion group. What does Laura mean? Check (✔) *True* or *False*.**

	True	False
1. Kevin can use a computer on the farm.	_____	_____
2. Laura is surprised about technology on a farm.	_____	_____

Laura Eastment, Argentina

What About YOU? **What is your opinion? Check (✔) *I agree* or *I disagree*.**

	I agree	I disagree
1. Computers are a part of everyone's life.	_____	_____
2. All students need to use computers.	_____	_____

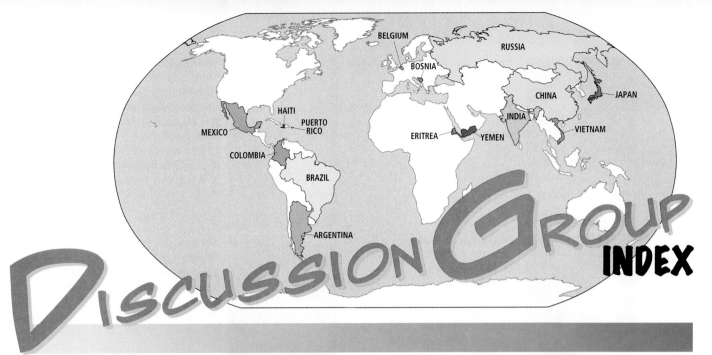

DISCUSSION GROUP INDEX

To find the students for the Discussion Group, signs about the CONNECT WITH ENGLISH television program were placed in universities and community centers in the Boston area. More than 100 people offered to participate. From this group, about 40 people auditioned on tape. They were asked questions like, "Where do you come from?" and, "How did you get to the United States?" The final 16 people were chosen because they told the most interesting stories, felt comfortable in front of the camera, and had clear speaking voices. The students did not have a script to read from. All of their stories are true, and they did not practice their lines.

**Roberto Arévalo
Colombia**

Roberto moved to the United States because he wanted to see more of the world. He arrived in 1981 and now works as a video producer. His wife is a doctor.

**Olga Baloueff
Belgium**

Olga lived in Belgium and in Zaire before she moved to the United States. She is currently going to graduate school in the Boston area, and she has a husband and a son.

**Nina Chen
China**

Nina was a teacher before she came to the United States in 1982. Nina thinks education is very important and is proud that both of her daughters have finished college.

**Ventha Danapalan
India**

Ventha came to the United States in 1992. Before he moved to Boston, he studied electrical engineering in Arizona.

**Laura Eastment
Argentina**

Laura moved to the United States from Argentina in 1969. She came to the United States to study agricultural engineering.

**Nisenat Gabrezgi
Eritrea**

Nisenat came to the United States in 1992. She says that her experiences in her new home are a lot like Rebecca's—except that Nisenat has the extra job of learning English!

Patrick Jerome
Haiti

Patrick was a filmmaker in Haiti before he moved to the United States in 1993. He attends college in the Boston area.

Nela Hosic
Bosnia

Nela had been in the United States only two months before she became a part of the Discussion Group. Her husband and two children moved with her, but her parents still live in Bosnia.

Abdul Khushafah
Yemen

Abdul left his home country of Yemen in 1984, where he worked as a carpenter. He is glad he made the decision to move. He now works as a designer.

Boris Levitin
Russia

Boris was born in Moscow, Russia. He lived in Israel before he moved to the United States in 1979 at the age of fifteen.

Lan Ma
China

Lan is from Beijing, China, and came to the United States in 1990 to continue her education. When she arrived in Boston she didn't know anybody, but now she is very happy to live there.

Raúl Méndez
Puerto Rico

Raúl is a developmental psychologist at a hospital in Boston. He still works in Puerto Rico three months a year, and he has two grandchildren who live there.

Casilda Nunes
Brazil

Casilda is in the United States to study English. She only planned to stay for six months, but when the Discussion Group was filmed, she had been in the U.S. for almost two years.

Yukiyoshi Ozawa
Japan

Yukiyoshi was actually born in San Francisco, California, but he was raised in Japan. He is now a college student in Boston. He came to live in the United States in 1995.

Hai B. Pho
Vietnam

Hai arrived in the United States over forty years ago. His family wanted him to continue his education in the U.S. He moved back to Vietnam in the 1970s, but now he lives near Boston.

Rosalba Solís
Mexico

Rosalba came from Mexico in 1978 to pursue her dream of becoming a jazz musician. Like Rebecca, she wanted to go to music school, and today she is a music teacher in Boston.

CHARACTER INDEX

This index includes the names of most of the characters who appear in CONNECT WITH ENGLISH, alphabetized by their first names.

Alberto Mendoza

San Francisco, California.
An architect who meets Rebecca in the desert.

Alex Mendoza

San Francisco, California.
Ramón's son and a student at the after-school program.

Angela Calud

San Francisco, California.
A nursing student. She lives at Nancy Shaw's house.

Bill Ellis

San Francisco, California.
A student at the San Francisco College of Music and Rebecca's friend.

Brendan & Anne Casey

Aurora, Illinois.
Rebecca and Kevin's uncle and aunt.

Carmen & Enrique Mendoza

San Francisco, California.
Alberto and Ramón's parents. They own the Casa Mendoza restaurant.

Edward Shaw

San Francisco, California.
A retired musician, he is Nancy Shaw's uncle. He lives in a nursing home.

Emma Washington

San Francisco, California.
The director of the after-school program where Rebecca works.

Frank Wells

Boston, Massachusetts.
Patrick Casey's friend.

Jack Sullivan

Boston, Massachusetts.
Sandy's boyfriend.

Kevin Casey

Boston, Massachusetts.
Patrick Casey's son and Rebecca's younger brother.

María Gómez

San Francisco, California.
The financial aid counselor at the San Francisco College of Music.

Matt Carlson

Boston, Massachusetts. Rebecca's boyfriend in Boston.

Melaku Tadesse

San Francisco, California. A business student. He lives at Nancy Shaw's house.

Molly Kelly

Boston, Massachusetts. Margaret Casey's sister, and Rebecca and Kevin's aunt.

Nancy Shaw

San Francisco, California. Rebecca's godmother. She runs a boarding house for students. Rebecca lives with her in San Francisco.

Patrick Casey

Boston, Massachusetts. Rebecca and Kevin's father. He is a retired firefighter.

Ramón Mendoza

San Francisco, California. Alex's father and Alberto's brother. He works at his parents' restaurant.

Rebecca Casey

Boston, Massachusetts and San Francisco, California. A music student with a dream. She moves from Boston to San Francisco to study music. She is Patrick's daughter and Kevin's older sister.

Sandy Dawson

Boston, Massachusetts. Rebecca's best friend and Jack's girlfriend.

Professor Thomas

San Francisco, California. One of Rebecca's professors at the San Francisco College of Music.

Mr. & Mrs. Wang

San Francisco, California. Vincent's parents. Mr. Wang owns a store in Chinatown.

Vincent Wang

San Francisco, California. Alex's best friend at the after-school program. He is the son of Mr. and Mrs. Wang.